THE SELF AS FIGHTER

SHLOMO KALO

THE SELF
AS FIGHTER

Translated by Anat Rekem

 St Paul Publications

St Paul Publications
Middlegreen, Slough SL3 6BT, United Kingdom

Copyright © St Paul Publications UK 1991

ISBN 085439 369 2

Cover design by Diana Girdwood

Printed by The Guernsey Press Co. Ltd., Guernsey, C.I.

St Paul Publications is an activity of the priests and brothers of
the Society of St Paul who proclaim the Gospel through the
media of social communication

Contents

A few words of explanation

This creation is pure literature without the sophisticated literary embellishment. It describes – as much as possible – eternity and the way to it.

Yitschak, the central character, represents the average spiritual disciple, progressing towards his destination through constant struggle with himself. In fact, Yitschak is a combination of a few characters taken from real life.

Some of the events described herein have actually occurred and others are likely to occur. Mr S is not you, me, he or she, in the same way he is – you, me, he and she.

1

A paper guide

Following the publication of my translations into Hebrew,[1] quite a few people, mostly young, turned to me asking for clarifications. I answered them as well as I could and usually that was as far as these particular acquaintances would go.

Yitschak's case deviated slightly from this routine. He claimed that my clarifications raised further important questions within himself and continued to ask for additional meetings until I rejected him.

He was not offended but continued to come uninvited anyway. He used to sit on the bench by the front gate, outside my place of work, waiting patiently until I came out. Then he would greet me and look at me with pleading eyes.

He was a tall, blue eyed young man aged about twenty-three or twenty-four with thick and somewhat curly hair. Sometimes he would only get my greeting in return for his long waiting, but sometimes when I had the time, I would invite him in and listen to his questions.

[1] *The Song of God, Bhagavad-Gita; Sayings of Buddha* – selected verses from "The way of truth" – (Dhammapada); *Shankara: Absolute Freedom* ("Crest-Jewels of discrimination" Viveka Chudamani); *Zen and Zen Sages in 128 Zen Talks; Tao Te Ching of Lao Tze; Patañjali Yoga Verses.*

One day in late summer I asked him, 'What do you really want from me?'

It was three o'clock in the afternoon. The room was filled with tools and books. Even the old ventilator didn't work. It was stifling hot.

Yitschak wet his lips with the tip of his tongue, looked up at me without moving his head, and spoke with a sigh.

'Individual guidance.'

'So find yourself a guide,' was my reply.

'I don't have one,' he said half accusing and half begging.

'And what about the books you have?' I asked referring to my translations. 'Shankara, Patanjali, Gautama Sakyamuni(Buddha)', I specified. 'They are the best of guides!'

'They are paper guides.'

'That's up to you.'

He straightened up a little and whispered back, 'And you.'

I went silent.

The minutes went by and soon added up to half an hour, and then to an hour. He was sitting in front of me. Tiny transparent drops of sweat grew thicker and heavier on his wide forehead and eventually dripped from the edge of his eyebrows and down his chin.

'In every man's heart lies his destined guide,' I said. 'Surely you remember the "Have you ever lost it" Zen dialogue?'[2]

'Of course,' he answered and continued hastily, 'in which Sekito answers the questions of Shiry the monk with "What do you want from me?" and Shiry

[2] From the Hebrew version of *Zen and Zen Sages*, D.A.T. Publications, Tel-Aviv, p. 46.

replies: "If I ask no questions how will I ever find the solution?" and Sekito, the guru, concludes the conversation with "Have you ever lost it?" '

'Do you see then?' I asked.

'Nevertheless,' Yitschak said, concealing a smile in his eyes, 'Shiry needed a guide…'

2

The tomorrow
which passed yesterday

Following that conversation, we started meeting at Yitschak's rented room or on the beach, as well as at my work place. We were strolling along the Tel-Aviv beach one day.

'What are you striving for?' I asked him.

'Self-realization.'

'You mean you are willing and prepared to devote yourself completely and wholeheartedly to...' I didn't complete my sentence.

Twilight was ending. The beach was covered with a mixture of shells and sand which gave out a monotonous creaking sound under our sandals as the soft breeze played with the short sleeves of our shirts.

'To what?' Yitschak urged me.

'To the cruellest of battles on earth.'

He did not respond.

The simultaneous creaks accompanied us for a little longer and then stopped as we went down to the Jaffa beach. We walked in absolute silence for a long time. The soft lines of the Bat-Yam beach appeared in the distance.

Suddenly Yitschak started quoting, 'The incomparable Buddha's teachings become comprehensible only after arduous exercises of discipline; by overcoming that which is the most difficult to overcome and by practising that which is the most difficult to practise. People of inferior nature and average intelligence are prevented from understanding any of this. All of their efforts are doomed to failure from the start.'

'You are strong in quotations,' I said, 'let's see you in deeds!'

I turned left and he followed me. We went out of the coastal area, quickly returning to the bustling centre of the city. The street lights were on. Under these pale lights, a stream of human beings rushed about, each going his own way.

'Can you pray?' I asked.

'What, for instance?'

'Any short prayer, a verse of the Psalms?'

'O Lord, my God, in thee I have taken refuge…'[3]

'And the rest?'

'I forgot.'

'Can you repeat it ten times?'

He smiled, 'Is that the test?'

'Half of it.'

'What's the other half?'

'The manner of praying,' I replied, standing still, and added, 'Do as I do!'

I turned to the kerb and chose a sufficiently lit spot, clear of cars and people, but fairly conspicuous. Then I went down on my knees, joined my hands together and with my face lifted up towards the sky, I said three times the whole verse of 'I will give thanks to the Lord with all my heart…'[4]

The people stared in amazement. Some fled, a few approached with an amused expression on their faces and made some sarcastic remarks. I stood up, approached Yitschak and said, 'Your turn!'

---

[3] Psalm 7:1.
[4] Psalm 86:12.

The look in his eyes was that of astonishment and panic. His face turned pale, his blue eyes seemed almost black. He made a movement with the upper part of his body but the rest of it just wouldn't obey him. He stood rigid in his place and after a few seconds stuttered, 'I can't, no, not now, not at the same place.'

I walked away. He ran after me, seizing my elbow with a sweaty, trembling hand. 'Please!' he said, 'I'm ready to go down on my knees, at the very same place,' and immediately ran to that same lighted spot. There he joined his hands together but did not lift them up, so the joined hands turned instantly into a jittery twist of curved fingers. Instead of lifting his head up to the sky, he was twisting it to the side in a pathetic and ridiculous manner. His lips moved quickly and before any of the passers-by could notice him, he was standing beside me, breathing heavily as though he had just completed a marathon.

'Next time I'll do it with greater perfection, please disregard that!'

Yitschak definitely amused me! I gave him a slap on the shoulder and burst into roars of laughter. The people around, who didn't understand the reason for my laughter, approached and looked at Yitschak who was smiling uncomfortably, like a schoolboy caught with a cigarette in his hand.

'Next time?' I said, still laughing myself to tears. 'When will that be? In five thousand years or one hundred thousand? What will be left then of this street or this city?'

'I mean tomorrow or the day after...' Yitschak muttered with embarrassment and gave apologetic looks to the passers-by who were stopping to stare at us because of my laughter.

'Man!' I said, 'Tomorrow or the day after passed yesterday. What you will not do today, you'll never be able to do!'

'I don't understand you,' Yitschak whispered.

'If you did, you'd be rushing to get down on your knees before every creature passing in this street in order to atone for the sin of omission you've just committed.'

'I promise there will be no more omissions!' he declared solemnly.

3

As the tiny cloud
to the endless sky

Yitschak's rented room was close by. We turned to
a wide, empty street and arrived at the foot of a tall
building with walls that were peeled by the stormy
winds from the sea.

The room had a small porch where we sat. Yitschak
disappeared into the darkness of a tiny kitchen and
returned with a tray, carrying two cups of tea, a few
apples and a couple of fairly old slices of corn bread.

After a long silence he said, 'I'm sorry I didn't do
what I should have done immediately and properly. Is
this the cruel battle?'

'Ah,' I answered, 'imagine you've arrived at the
foot of a lofty mountain with the intention of removing
it. The first thing you'd have to do is scratch a few tiny
little stones with your finger nails in order to determine the nature of the mountain you are going to fight
against. Can you say that by doing so you have
already removed it?'

He was listening most attentively. After a few
minutes, I added, 'Nevertheless, it's the first step
towards achieving the goal. This is the head start
without which you will never get to the beginning,
not to mention the goal itself.'

'What was the purpose of kneeling down?'
Yitschak asked.

'Preparation for the opening of the battle.'

'Against who?'

'Against your greatest, sharpest and cruellest enemy on earth.'

'Who is my "greatest, sharpest and cruellest enemy on earth"?'

'The "I".'

'Is it ever possible to vanquish the "I"?'

'It exists in order to be vanquished, that is its purpose.'

'Have you vanquished the "I"?' Yitschak asked, suppressing a troubling thought which suggested that his question was impertinent.

'The "I" exists in order be vanquished,' I replied.

'Sir,' he stressed, 'my question is, have *you* vanquished the "I"?'

'It exists in order to be vanquished.'

'I understood you very well: The "I" exists in order to be vanquished. But for heaven's sake, answer my question: have you yourself vanquished it?'

'The "I" exists in order be vanquished.'

He looked around helplessly, pondered for a minute and then asked decisively, 'Who are you, Sir?'

'I don't know,' I answered.

I have never been interested in S who was sitting in the dimness of Yitschak's room and communicating my answers. Who is he? A paper puppet? An endless number of illusory atoms, combined to form a transitory appearance, just as fictional? What is he to me? And the one sitting beside him, isn't he his twin brother, emerging from the imagination and returning to it in a fleeting moment? What are they to me? A certain relation – as the drops of the ocean's wave, scattered in the air, to the ocean itself; as the tiny cloud to the endless sky; as the dead nails or hair to their living owner.

17

For S that was clear but not for Yitschak. For him, the endless ocean seemed to be a single bubble of water, flying into the air and ultimately bursting, vanishing as if it had never existed.

4
The keys
of the universe

'Oh sir,' I heard Yitschak murmuring, 'I was asking you about the prayer... I can see you're already listening to me. You sank into some sort of... meditation. I was asking about prayer: is it absolutely indispensable in the fight against the "I"? Isn't it possible to use something else instead, like a poem or a song or whatever comes into your mind?'

'Indeed you can, and sometime there's no escape from saying something else, like a poem, a song, a proverb or just a group of unrelated words. But prayer has an enormous power which no poem, song, proverb or word has, but not everyone is likely to benefit from the power accumulated in prayer.'

'Who is likely to benefit from the power accumulated in prayer?'

I studied him as the darkness in the room thickened. I could see him very well but I doubt if he saw me. He certainly felt my eyes focused on him. I refrained from asking him to put on the light, for this tension I created by examining him would be beneficial for him in the future, when he would come to forge his vigilance.

'Only a certain kind of people are likely to activate the power accumulated in a prayer and uproot mountains with its aid.' My eyes wandered over my companion's curls. His tension increased and consequently the expression on his face changed to that of a primitive creature, a kind of Indian whose red face was deeply carved with wrinkles.

'Who are they?' asked Yitschak.

'Those possessing absolute faith. "The Lord is near to all who call upon him, to all who call upon him in truth."'[5] I quoted and added, 'This is a definitive declaration which is all truth.'

'Those people are few,' said Yitschak with a sigh.

'Few,' I agreed.

'I wouldn't say I'm a man of faith,' declared Yitschak. 'How does prayer work?'

'Like a car key. In order to set your car in motion you need a key. Once you've placed the right key into the appropriate keyhole, the car is awakened from its frozen state and will run at any speed and direction you desire. We are surrounded by wide layers of energy, loads of charges, each one as powerful as hundreds of nuclear bombs; each of them has its own particular activating key. One of those keys is prayer – the prayer of a man saturated with strong faith. The key is in his hands. The moment he wishes, he can activate it and then watch wonders! Mountains are displaced, the sun is stopped in its orbit, the universe explodes...'

'But as has been said before,' Yitschak saw fit to repeat his remark, 'those people are very few...!'

'Very few,' I agreed. 'In order to become *a man of absolute faith* one must go through such trials, they will not leave a trace of any desire in him, whether constructive or destructive. The men of absolute faith are men of silence. The key placed in their hands rusts from lack of use.'

[5] Psalm 145:18.

'Why?'

'Because they know the futility of power and the folly of rulership, for they are the people who have vanquished the temptation of power and rulership, and therefore were given the keys of the universe. If they wish they can destroy or establish it. At their wish they can let it roll on to where it was destined to roll, and this is exactly what they do – let the universe roll on to where it was meant to roll. The keys have been entrusted to their hands for safekeeping.'

'What purpose have these exceptional people?' asked Yitschak.

'To be themselves, that is, eternity and infinity, absolute freedom. And from the moment those keys were put into their hands it is a sign that they have achieved their goal.'

'Who put the keys into their hands?'

'They themselves.'

Yitschak got up and turned the light on in order to see the expression on my face.

'Sir,' he said quietly and seriously, 'I don't understand you!'

'The human beings existing in this universe are all perfect. The greatest majority of them are unaware of that. A tiny number seek to achieve awareness and even a tinier number achieve it. Then, they realize that they have never been anything but one infinite integrity and that the keys of the universe were in their hands from time immemorial, but they couldn't see it. From the moment this discernment is achieved, you might say that this very same entity passes the keys of the universe from itself to itself. That's why it's good to pray, even if you are sure you are not a man of absolute faith. It's possible that all of a sudden something will flicker and you'll be awakened to knowing the truth. It is like searching for a needle in

21

a haystack of infinite size in total darkness. The probability that the searching fingers will touch that needle is almost zero. Nevertheless, it's possible and has happened before, not once or twice, but not much more than that; approximately once in a million and in certain generations even less than that.'

'What happens when the prayer achieves its purpose?'

'You achieve what you asked for.'

'If I asked for mountains to be moved?'

'They will be moved.'

'But the people of absolute faith, who are aware of themselves, do not ask for such things, do they?'

'He who asks for mountains to be moved has yet to achieve absolute faith, but he who wishes to achieve awareness will gain it, and with it absolute faith, pure and clear of the smallest of doubts.'

I disconnected again.

It was 10 p.m. when I noticed Yitschak had fallen asleep on his chair. Silently I left the room.

5
He

As usual, S woke up early in the morning to the bluish twilight, not yet dawn. Since he is aware of me, he was nothing but pure, endless happiness: happiness impossible to describe with the means available to flesh and blood.

S has abolished himself and therefore gained me. He is still called by his name and still answers his callers, but it isn't him, it is I who operate him; he and I are one.

S does not exist but in the eyes of the non-existent: all those imaginary shapes and forms regarding themselves as living creatures whose whole essence is death.

S's mortal eyes absorb the brightness of the rising sun which is nothing but a pale and somewhat distorted reflection of my eternal light. S is conscious of me and therefore unimpressed by the dawn. His eyes always see nothing but me – The Eternal Happiness, The Perfect Light. I am one with him as I am one with the whole universe. But the universe has not yet realized this and therefore it is saturated with agony and futility.

S has won and has become enlightened. He is out of reach of the imaginary creatures of all kinds. He has ceased to be an imaginary creature; he has become absolute freedom. His 'I' is nothing but me. But I am the only one capable of grasping the meaning of these words, even though it was not I who wrote them, for I do not do a thing in the literal sense of the word, I do not speak, eat, construct or destroy etc., but nothing would be done without me. I am in everything and everything is in me and I am the only one who's aware of that.

Every man has the chance of reaching me and of realizing himself within me, but very few will.

There are human beings who develop and reach the world called supreme which is also populated by a variety of images. They turn into more subtle and sublime entities like an industrious clerk ascending to the rank of a manager. But that doesn't mean they have reached me, for even the most sublime creatures or entities are subjected to changes. Even the supreme world is at the mercy of constructive and destructive forces, just like this world. The supreme world is not the object of the Creation or an end in itself; I am the object of the Creation and at the same time, the source of all created things.

He who has reached me would be forever free of change and will not taste death. He and I are one, that is, he becomes absolute freedom, pure love, perfect happiness and eternal light – the one and only ever-lasting reality.

6

Getting prepared

Yitschak came to pick me up in an old Peugeot car he had just bought and we drove to the Palmachim beach. Due to the scarcity of visitors on this beach, it remained clean and the water, lapping the mixture of sand and gravel, was clearer than in other familiar places.

Yitschak had brought a thermos of hot tea and a small bag containing apples and sandwiches of cheese and tomato.

'Let's pray.' I put my palm on his hand that had already pulled out a thick sandwich.

He left the sandwich, straightened up, joined his palms and closed his eyes, murmuring something with his lips.

When we finished, he attempted to start a conversation but I lifted my finger to stop him.

I ate calmly. Yitschak tried to imitate me. He sliced a small piece and chewed it slowly, but very soon got carried away by the fierce turbulence of his thoughts. His self-vigilance was lost and his jaws chewed in an ever increasing rhythm. He finished his portion within five minutes while I finished mine a quarter of an hour later. We did not utter a word during all of this time.

After returning the washed dishes back to

Yitschak's knapsack I lay down on the sand and the young man asked me, 'All those enormously powerful energies you mentioned, how is it they weren't activated until now, inadvertently or deliberately?'

'They were.'

'And the universe still exists?'

'And will in the future.'

'Please explain!'

'Try to understand: every force and energy is nothing but an illusion, a mere illusion. The force, energy and charge are nothing but a symbol of constant change. They cause change, that is, constructing or destroying and in themselves are given to change – becoming bigger or smaller. But they are not real. The changeless is real. And you cannot perceive this with tools which in themselves are constantly changing.'

'Which tools?'

'The only tools we have – consciousness, thought, emotion and will.'

'But these energies destroy an entire universe!'

'The energies destroy the universe and reconstruct it as well. Sometimes they are activated by those who deciphered their code and sometimes they activate themselves, but still they are forever changing. Compared with the one reality, as mentioned before, they are nothing but a mere illusion, a shadow of things. The reality is Eternity.'

'What should one do in order to reach that reality?'

'In order to reach that reality we must bring the energies to a perfect neutralization. Then, being checked by each other, they melt away and vanish like a nightmare which had lasted a million years and all at once has come to an end. Then, through the last cloud of illusion, the pure light of the eternal reality will shine. The worthy one who has achieved it will never again know any futile sorrow or passing pleasure. He is one with himself forever. In order to achieve it, you need to bring the energies to the neutralizing "great clash".'

'That means,' Yitschak tried to interpret, 'that it is essential to gain control over the energies.'

'To become free of them. And one of the best ways to do that is prayer.'

'Are there other ways?'

'It is possible to reach the "great clash" by evading it. You evade the energies until you disconnect from them and their influence. That means you seclude yourself – withdraw from the world and all its temptations. The safest way is contemplation.'

'Why is contemplation the safest way?'

'Because not only does it bring about the "great clash", but checks it as well.'

'I don't understand.'

'The point is not to bring about the "great clash" or make it happen, but not to miss it. Contemplation is a way of nurturing the highest degree of vigilance which is needed in order not to miss the "great clash". A man who brought about the "great clash" or made it happen and missed it, returns from his journey empty-handed.'

'How do you miss the "great clash"?'

'You don't notice it when it happens. It comes suddenly, in a flash, without warning. For a split second the light will flash. If you've noticed it, it is eternally yours, but if you've missed it, you'll go right back to the starting point of your journey towards it. Contemplation "checks" the "great clash" by increasing the vigilance of its followers to the greatest extent possible. He who has been diligent with his contemplation will not miss the "great clash".'

'Which is the shortest route to the "great clash"?'

'All routes are liable to lengthen or shorten, depending upon their follower, his devotion and perseverance. A route which has been shortened other than by devotion and perseverance is dangerous.'

'Why?'

'The hasty one might get swept away by the fierce maelstrom of the activated energies. More precisely, he might be tempted by one of them and gain control over it because he is not aware of its being an illusion. The actual outcome in such a case is enslave-ment to that energy that is "controlled" so to speak. That means, returning to the enslavement of the illusion.'

'Is that why those possessing absolute faith do not activate the energies?'

'Yes, they see the real essence of the energies – they recognize them as an illusion and therefore turn away from them.'

'Mr S,' Yitschak said solemnly, 'I choose the shortest and safest way! Please help me!'

'Help yourself!' I said provocatively.

'And what will you do?'

'Enjoy God's glorious world!' My laughter reverberated loudly and clearly. Yitschak smiled with embarrassment. After a few minutes I turned to him and said, 'You've started to pray, haven't you?'

'Yes.'

'Go on then, but now change the viewpoint.'

'Which viewpoint?'

'Of the prayer. Look at it from a different angle,' and to his silent question I added, 'You do want to bring about the "great clash", don't you?' He nodded in agreement.

'See the absolute in the divinity,' I said.

'What is the meaning of "the absolute"?'

28

'That which is beyond the energies and yet nothing exists outside of it.'

'It's hard to imagine such a thing.'

'Make an effort. Be diligent. And another thing – contemplate twice a day. First just try to clear your mind of any thoughts…'

'How can one clear his mind of any thoughts?' Yitschak interrupted.

'Any way one finds convenient. Every human charge of energy, that is, every person, has his own convenient way of fighting his thought. Some let their thought-waves pass through their mind and some stop them at any possible point... I will also give you a suitable tool for letting them pass through or stopping them.'

'A mantra?'

'Sort of.'

I shook myself off S and took in Yitschak – a confusion of thought waves, all colours of the rainbow of contradicting emotions... Somewhere out there passed a curved line, like a black artery of carnal desire. 'This is the point' was the sentence that flashed through my mind. I turned to Yitschak:

'Repeat constantly "Absolute Purity".'

'Absolute Purity,' Yitschak repeated after me.

'Dedicate a special time for this twice a day. Start ten minutes before sunrise and ten minutes before sunset, each time for half an hour, and try to see the meaning of this expression.'

'Absolute Purity?'

'Yes, Absolute Purity. This is one way of describing the Divinity or Absolute. It is one of the most fitting expressions for the one reality which stands beyond the energies, remember that!'

'And what of the fight against the "I"?'

'This is it.'

'I'm already fighting it?'

I looked at him with exaggerated amazement and asked, 'When you go to war, do you open the windows of your house and start shooting?'

'If I was taken by surprise,' he replied, trying to justify his question.

'If you were surprised to the point where you were forced to defend yourself from your very own house, then your position is the worst possible and your hours are few.'

'And if the "I" should attack suddenly...?'

'If the "I" were to attack you right now, you would be like a man who's forced to shoot the enemy surrounding him, from the windows of his house... but this is not your case, thank God... you are just getting prepared for battle.'

'I beg your pardon sir, is the "I" attacking?'

'The minute he feels he is being attacked.'

'And what if the person who's supposed to fight him didn't yet manage to prepare himself?'

'The attack of the "I" will crush him. That person will be completely shattered and will remain within the enslavement of the "I" for many years.'

'How many?'

'A hundred thousand. Half a million. Anyway, his progress is stopped and that's why it's important that only a person who is sufficiently developed will fight the "I".'

'Am I sufficiently developed?'

'You have a few of the requirements. It's possible to bet on you,' I replied with a mischievous smile, since I had revealed to him a bit more than he should know, as he might nurture an impeding self-confidence. In order to change the subject I added, 'At the moment you are getting prepared for battle. Taking an inventory, straightening lines, trying to obtain and fill up what's missing... and you'll be doing well if these things are not revealed to your enemy – the "I" within you.'

'How is that possible?'

'It's possible. You must act as if you know nothing and yet prepare. Stop asking useless questions; they do nothing but harm. Delve into what you've been told and try to understand it.'

'In conclusion...?' Yitschak hesitated.

'Pray to achieve absolute faith. Contemplate twice a day. And repeat at every opportunity, place and situation the two redeeming words. Do not belittle them, for they are very powerful, as powerful as nuclear bombs. Activate them relentlessly, for the opponent confronting you is getting ready for battle as well and he is ruthless... That's why it is essential to use all the power you possess against him. Accumulate it and activate it.'

And with these words, that were uttered emphatically, I disconnected.

7

The seed fable

When the twilight had deepened, I awakened
Yitschak, who was lying on the clean sand, snoozing
in the caressing sea breeze.

'If you continue this way you will fail shame-
fully!' I cried into his ear.

He was startled and sprang up immediately, trying
to look alert in order to prove my statement wrong.
But all of this did not atone for his sin.

'You won't get very far if you continue to doze
off!'

'I'm sorry! I'm very sorry! It won't happen again!'
he apologized and vowed, and yet tried to get back at
me with a sarcastic remark, '*Your Honour* had also
been snatched away to some distant star, what was I
supposed to do?'

'Join *His Honour*!' I replied.

'I have not yet learned the art of walking among
the stars.'

'Then learn. You can achieve anything you wish
to. And please, enough justifications!' I hushed him
with a decisively final hand movement. 'Listen,' I
emphasized, 'listen carefully! In a little while your
enemy will send his first sign of noticing you…'

'Is he noticing me as well?' Yitschak interrupted,
intrigued.

'And what did you think, that he dozes off like

you?' I commented and continued, 'In a little while, one of his scouts will be here. He will try to examine your nature. If you rout him, you will have made a significant step ahead. But if he routs you, then he has made progress at your expense.'

'What you're saying isn't very clear to me but I'm ready and prepared… Is he going to take the form of a thought, emotion or desire…'

'No, not yet,' I revealed and explained, 'You are not yet mature enough for that… You will be granted something very naïve, a kids' game. Thoughts, as you know, are deadly weapons of the finest kind. We are talking about something different…'

'What, exactly?'

'You will soon see.'

'How should I behave?'

'Don't be routed.'

'You are just putting me on!' Yitschak said with a nervous giggle and started surveying the area thoroughly.

I moved away until we were about twenty metres apart. Out of the thickening darkness came the figure of a great big bulldog. Its sluggish walk indicated that it wasn't hungry and probably was out for a pleasure walk. Since I stood in its way, it approached me and stared at me with bloodshot eyes. Its moist tongue was shaking and trembling rapidly. I didn't respond. It came closer until its snout almost touched my chin and then all of a sudden turned back and ran away from me.

At first it seemed as if the dog did not notice Yitschak. It walked past him and went on its way, shaking its heavy body rhythmically. It went a few metres further away from him, then stood still as if reconsidering, turned around slowly and levelled its gaze at Yitschak. Its panting tongue hung between white cuspids, covered with foam. The dog walked heavily towards Yitschak's silhouette which crumpled at first but then straightened up a little to face the expected confrontation. As the dog moved, the shapely muscles of its body were emphasized under its shining brown skin. The animal quickened its step and all at once stood in front of Yitschak, who was standing still. The dog wrinkled its flattened nose, exposed its sharp teeth, stretched backwards as though about to leap, then uttered a frightening growl, leaped forward... and stopped.

Yitschak froze. He was either in a state of shock or just standing firmly against the attacker.

The dog relaxed, moistened its muzzle with its tongue, glanced away sadly and went on its way.

The silhouette of the man sitting on the sand relaxed. The animal was striding off carelessly as if to say, 'I found no interest in you.' Then all of a sudden it turned back and ran madly towards Yitschak.

Then like a flash Yitschak was at the top of the hill with the dog running after him. He went down the other side, made a wide turn and ran towards me at the speed of an Olympic sprinter. The dog reached him, its snout almost touching his seat. The chase ended.

The dog had either had enough or wanted to deal with something else that had bothered it. It stood still, sniffing the ground and picked up a pale object about the size of a palm. It started tearing it to pieces with its front paws and teeth, and then took off.

Yitschak was rolling beside me, breathing like a broken locomotive. The strong smell of sweat filled the air. He pushed me in the direction that the dog was liable to reappear from, so that I would shelter him from it.

'Ha ha ha ha!' I burst out laughing. 'Ha ha ha ha!' I rolled in the sand, laughing without restraint.

Yitschak, who was still breathing heavily and shivering all over, sat nearby and stared at me with eyes that almost popped out of their sockets.

'What a fine chase!' I started roaring with laughter again in a voice that shook the rocks. 'What a fine chase!'

'Have... you... gone... mad...?' stuttered Yitschak.

'Ha ha ha...' was my response.

Suddenly Yitschak began weeping bitterly, a spontaneous pitiful weeping that shook his whole body. It was the manifestation of frustration blended with great strain, suppressed anger and a poignant feeling of insult, despair and defeat.

I went close to him, put my hands on his shoulders and gave him a good shake, 'Enough,' I said, 'enough. That's all you need now, to be pitying yourself like a hypochondriac old maid!'

He tried to restrain himself, fastened his lips to the point of distortion, clenched his fists and eventually seemed to succeed since his whimpers turned into hiccups that gradually faded.

'Listen,' I said, 'maybe this whole thing is not for you. Not every acorn grows into a tree. You still have the choice. You can turn back, there's no harm in that. Later on you'll get hurt and suffer even more. Let's go home where you can reconsider the whole thing.'

Yitschak calmed down. He stood up in the darkness and staggered towards the road where he had parked his car. As I got up after him, I realized the nature of the object that the dog had been worrying. It was a piece of Yitschak's trousers.

While Yitschak started his car, I heard him whispering close to my ear, 'I'm not backing out, I've decided, I'll go all the way!'

After driving for a while in complete silence, Yitschak mustered the courage to say, 'If you had noticed, the score at the moment is a tie – one:one,' and hurried to explain: 'When the dog sniffed me I didn't move, not even a millimetre. Only its tactics were cunning... turning back when I least expected it! By the way, who sent it?'

He suspected that somehow I had organized the show.

'You suppose I had something to do with it?'

'The dog recognized you. It sniffed you a little and ran off...'

'Do you want to know the truth?' I turned to him with a wide smile and after a moment of silence revealed, 'You are the one who brought it on yourself!'

We had just gone out onto the highway which was bright with neon lights. Yitschak was supposed to accelerate and indeed did so. He pressed the accelerator lightly; the car made half a leap and then suddenly stopped in a frightening scream of brakes.

'Who brought the dog?' Yitschak leaned towards me, trying to make sure he heard me right.

'You.' I answered calmly.

'You are trying to drive me crazy!' Underneath his firm voice the sound of weeping began to rise. He made an effort to conceal it.

'Listen here my boy!' I turned firmly back to him. 'You are yourself and your enemy at the same time. The sublime "self" you set out to reach in order to fulfil yourself is you, and the "I" standing in its way is also you. As long as the lower "I" controls you, you are your most bitter enemy. Once the inferior "I" is defeated, out you go from slavery to freedom. This is indeed hard to understand.'

'How have I brought that damned bulldog upon myself?' insisted Yitschak. 'I demand an explanation!'

36

'We'll try to provide you with one,' I replied and made an attempt at making up a fable. 'When a seed buried in the ground decides to grow and come out into the open air, it releases certain juices which gnaw at its shell. For the seed, these juices seem like enemies because they eat and consume it, eventually putting an end to its existence as a seed. On the other hand, it caused this itself by making the decision to turn from a seed buried in the darkness of the earth, into a plant ascending into the open air. From the moment a person decides to attain fulfilment, he brings plenty of enemies upon himself. They serve no other purpose than to gnaw and consume his peel in order to put an end to his existence as a transient creature in a fantasy world.'

'I want to know how my thought of fulfilment brought the bulldog,' Yitschak persisted.

'In the illusory world of the energies everything is interconnected, although no one is clearly aware of that. The imaginary "I" will take on any form it regards suitable, ordinary or extraordinary, in order to stimulate fear, hatred, jealousy, greed, passion or pride…'

'In my case it took the form of a bulldog,' Yitschak remarked, informing me that he understood and was following my speech.

'Might have taken the shape of a bulldog,' I corrected, emphasizing the word 'might', 'but in that particular case it didn't.'

'Then who brought the bulldog?'

'I already told you, you brought it on yourself. You didn't take on the shape of a bulldog but activated it.'

'Such efficiency!'

'Such economy!' I said and went on explaining, 'in order to be yourself, you must conquer yourself.

Without a fight and victory you will remain you, that is, the pseudo "I".

It is you then who stimulate your "juices" to put an end to your peel. In a sense, you might say it is you provoking yourself, in order that this "I" of yours might end your present existence, with which you are revolted, from the genuine feeling that it is nothing but an illusion.'

'Why aren't the rest of the people feeling like me?'

'That has to do with the stage of their evolution. Not every snake sheds its skin, only the one whose time has come and whose skin has burst, showing the new skin underneath. The fruit must first ripen, then fall into the appropriate soil in a suitable temperature and humidity for the seed to "occur" to it to turn into a plant. It will not "occur" to the seed to dream of the shape of a plant and open air as long as the appropriate conditions are not present. The sprout of such a thought exists of course in the seed and this is actually the seed itself. The seed was predestined to turn into a plant but this will occur to it only at a certain stage of its evolution, at a certain level of its maturity and in the appropriate conditions.'

'What would happen if the seed started dreaming of becoming a plant before the appropriate stage of evolution and the suitable circumstances had been achieved?'

'It would be an aborted seed, consumed before its time – it would never become a plant. But such cases are very rare. There are unseen mechanisms in the seed which are responsible for transmitting the external and internal signs. Only when those mechanisms inform the seed of the suitable time does the seed raise the idea of becoming a plant. This idea activates its "enemies" who in actual fact are itself. They consume its peel and end its existence as a seed in order to turn it into a plant.'

Moving heavily, Yitschak restarted his car and after a few lukewarm resistant coughs, it sounded its familiar rumble. We were soon part of the bustling traffic of the city.

'Why all the complexity? And how come it's all known to you?' Yitschak asked.

'Tonight's broadcast is over!' I said decisively, opening the window and looking at the dense crowd streaming on the pavements on both sides of the boulevard.

Since the dog had bitten Yitschak he went to the Veterinary Control Authority, which conducted an investigation in order to find the dog, but failed. No one in the nearby kibbutz or villages had noticed a stray bulldog. Of the two bulldogs owned by one of the suspected villages, solid testimonies were given that on that day they did not leave the village area.

Because of the fear of rabies, Yitschak's relatives and friends started pressing him to take the seventeen immunization shots. He came to me for advice.

'This time I'll get professional advice,' he remarked, referring to my profession.

'I will point out a few facts to you,' I said. 'A: one out of five thousand people receiving the seventeen immunization shots has damage to the central nervous system or dies as a result of the shots. B: only three out of a hundred people bitten by a mad dog, catch the rabies virus. C: the untreated infected die and the treated don't always stay alive. D: if the dog had rabies it's reasonable to assume he would have bitten me as well.'

Yitschak decided against getting the immunization shots. This might have ensured him a long life, had it been decreed that he was to live long.

39

8
To look
in order to see

We were sitting silently in Yitschak's room when he suddenly asked a question that had probably been bothering him all week, 'How did you know the dog was about to come?'

'I didn't know – I saw.'

'Why didn't I see?'

'Because you weren't looking!'

'I looked, just like you. Especially after your warning. I examined the area up and down even more thoroughly than you!'

'You examined, but didn't look!'

'What is the meaning of *to look*?'

'Looking in order to see. You didn't look in order to see, or else you would have seen. He who looks in order to see – sees.'

'How do you look in order to see?'

'Look,' I said indicating the point between his eyebrows, 'that's where the light of sight emanates from. When you activate it, you see. You see what's coming and what is about to come. You see what stands light-years away from where you are.'

'How do you activate this light of sight?'

'In order for a sooty flashlight to illuminate, you need to remove the soot from its lens.'

Yitschak looked at me, lowered his eyes, then

looked back at me and, rubbing his forehead at the point between his eyebrows, finally said, 'I can't see any trace of soot!'

'But I do.'

'Maybe you could clean it for me so that I'll be able to see?' he said, half joking and half begging.

'Only you can clean your own soot.'

'How do you do that?'

'You remove the bulk of conflicting thought-waves, the blur of feeble desires, the hidden currents of shady passions and the vain beauty of the emotions, and then you see – from one end of the world to the other.'

9

Who pardons whom

At that meeting, Yitschak asked whether he could change the timing of the pre-sunset contemplation.

'Why?' I asked him.

'Because one of the neighbours has bought a motorcycle and just as I sit down to contemplate he revs the engine to full power... the noise is deafening... it's impossible to concentrate. Instead you get...'

'What?' I urged.

'Angry,' he admitted and added, 'I tried to overcome this but the outcome is the opposite – the anger grows and takes over...'

'The anger over what?'

'The noise, of course, and the neighbour. I would prefer a different time.'

'Tomorrow,' I said, 'and only tomorrow, you will sit and contemplate a little later, when the noise has stopped. When the noise starts, you will go downstairs to your neighbour and ask for his forgiveness.'

'ME?' Yitschak stiffened and looked at me severely. We were drinking tea on his porch. The soft evening sky was studded with friendly twinkling stars.

'Why should I?' he asked, demanding an explanation.

'You will go downstairs at the time of the noise and ask your neighbour's pardon. Then, you will return and contemplate. That's what you will do tomorrow, and the day after tomorrow – back to your regular time, ten minutes before sunset.'

He thought it over while I drank my hot tea made of fragrant herbs from Galilee. He reached a conclusion.

'Mr S, will you please explain to me why I should ask my neighbour's pardon when he is the one who's disturbing *me*?' he stressed the word *me*, pointing his thumb at his chest.

'For being angry with him.'

'He should ask my forgiveness!'

'Try to understand,' I said, 'your neighbour did not go out in search of enlightenment but he serves as an auxiliary means to those who have. An auxiliary means which is not used properly will become an obstacle. You must consider this carefully. So go to him and ask his forgiveness.'

'He will surely ask the reason for this apology,' Yitschak said. He was softening a little.

'Tell him.'

'What?'

'That it's because he aroused your anger.'

'Is that something one should ask forgiveness for?'

'Absolutely. Your anger has hurt him the same way an excellent boxer might hurt a gentle child. His soul which contains a pure element and a certain beauty, has been distorted and deformed as a result of your anger.'

'I don't quite understand you…'

'Imagine that someone splashed concentrated acid on a gentle young lady who arouses sublime emotions within those who see her. Her refined beauty is totally ruined. Don't you think that the one who threw the acid should humbly ask for her forgiveness?'

43

'I will appear extremely weird in my neighbour's eyes, to say the least… I doubt if he will accept my apology at all.'

'You do your duty.'

'Is this really my duty?'

'As a spiritual disciple, yes.'

After a short silence, Yitschak spoke, 'Then anger deforms the world.'

'That's why it looks the way it does.'

'Nevertheless, the world is beautiful.'

'*Nevertheless*. Imagine how it would have looked without anger!'

'How?'

'Its beauty would have been close to the divine beauty.'

'He who's pure and free of anger sees this beauty?'

'He is a part of it,' I said with a wide smile that was shared by Yitschak. At that moment our faces lit up as we were united by soft laughter.

10
Fundamental courtesy...

A week later when we were sitting on Yitschak's porch, he told me, 'I went downstairs, as you advised me, and asked the noisy neighbour for his forgiveness. At first he thought he didn't hear me right and asked me to repeat what I had said. And so I did, quite clearly. "Forgiveness?" he asked, leaning towards me. "What for?" "For being angry with you," I said, and in order to clear any doubt he might have had, I explained, "When you made that noise, I got angry... please forgive me." He froze for a moment as if petrified or shocked and then hissed, "Get out of here! You moon-walker, get out!"' Yitschak concluded, 'Since then, the noise has become louder and longer.'

'It's because you weren't sincere.'

'Don't ask me to go and beg pardon again,' Yitschak warned.

I looked at the big red apples which lay on a large and unique China plate.

'Where does that plate come from?' I asked.

The expression on Yitschak's face changed. The tense lines relaxed and his eyes were lit up as he explained in a deep, quiet voice, 'This is a Chinese plate from the eighteenth century that my great-grandfather acquired during one of his travels. He was a well-known geologist who lived in China for some time. This plate was passed down to my grandfather, then to my father, and now it has come to me. According to the story, a mandarin who was the governor of the Tong-King region was its first owner but a rioting mob killed him in his palace. The plate changed hands a few times before it reached an antique dealer in Shanghai from whom my great-grandfather bought it.'

I looked at the delicate painting depicting a spacious, well-cultivated courtyard with tall trees and a pond, and two Chinese ladies leaning against one another. A strange structure, probably a palace, stood in the distance and in the pond's clear waters half a dozen fish were painted with magnificent vividness.

'Usually the plate hangs on the wall,' said Yitschak, pointing to a tiny hanger on the back of the plate, 'but in the event of an honourable guest...' He didn't complete his sentence.

'About this neighbour of yours,' I said, taking a red apple and rubbing it between my palms, 'Do you see him on other occasions?'

'Every morning at seven-thirty, at the front door of the building; we both go out to work at the same time.'

I peeled the apple, cut it up and took a slice. It was fresh, juicy and tasty.

'Do you greet each other?' I asked.

'Before the "apology" we used to nod at one another but now we absolutely ignore each other.'

'Starting from tomorrow, you will greet him with a wide and sincere smile. You can make as much effort as you please! Keep in mind that from the Absolute's point of view, he is but your twin brother, equal to you in everything. In fact, you, he and I are the very same thing. Your anger with him is anger over yourself… Don't be angry with yourself. Show yourself some mercy.'

'Is that the fight against the "I"?'

'This is fundamental courtesy!'

11

...And the outcome

At our next meeting Yitschak asked, 'How long should a contemplation session last?'

'At least ten minutes.'

'And at most?'

'There is not limit. This applies to the contemplation itself, which is carried out sitting properly – with body, head and neck held erect.'

'Is that the principle of sitting?'

'That's all. The crossed legs, posture of the hands and all the rest is unimportant. An erect upper part of the body ensures clear and lucid thinking.'

'By the way,' Yitschak recalled, 'there are no more interruptions.'

'What interruptions?'

'The guy stopped making the noise. I greeted him a few times with a "wide and sincere smile" and once even helped him start his motorcycle and there's no more noise,' he said, looking at me out of the corner of his eye. 'I helped myself and the self responded positively,' he concluded with apparent satisfaction as a wide smile spread all over his face.

12

A lesson on greed

As usual, before sunset Yitschak and I went out to the narrow, polluted beach of Tel-Aviv. The tar which stuck to our sandals was impossible to scrape off. We walked a certain distance, went up onto the noisy, bustling road and then back to the wider, much cleaner, beach of Jaffa. As we were walking, the word 'greed' came to my mind. It stood out with such persistent clarity that I could only give it my undivided attention. Then it was gone.

After a few even steps I settled down on a comfortable rock, facing the sea. Yitschak sat beside me. Our eyes wandered over the soft, friendly waves while the gentle, cool breeze blew pleasantly. The summer was bidding us farewell.

'What do you know of greed?' I started with a question.

'It is one of the attributes of the inferior "I". He who has attained enlightenment is free of it, or as Sri Krishna said: "He looks upon a lump of earth, a stone and a piece of gold with an equal eye,"'[6] Yitschak quoted.

[6] A.C. Bhaktivedanta Swami Prabhupada, *Bhagavad-Gita* 'As It Is', p. 704.

'"And is equal towards the desirable and the undesirable,"'[7] I completed the quote, and then added, 'Greed is the solid foundation of the imaginary "I"; it is its central pillar. The source of every desire is greed. In fact, the world of illusion exists, thanks to greed.'

'How is that?' Yitschak demanded an interpretations.

'Greed is the eye witness to the existence of the illusionary world. Without it, the world of illusion would collapse as castles in the air do, once the imagination – their creator – melts away and disappears. Greed is that facet of the illusionary world which looks up to it with desire, for the world of illusion has actually created greed.'

'The illusionary world has created greed – greed has created the world of illusion?'

I grinned, 'Yitschak, you are progressing!' I noted. 'You have grasped the philosophical principle of the illusionary world.'

'A vicious circle,' concluded Yitschak.

'A vicious circle,' I agreed.

'Why was it created in the first place?'

'A day will come when you'll stop asking.'

'Will I stop asking, or will I know?'

'One day the knowledge you are seeking will seem ridiculous to you.'

'Is it really ridiculous?'

'Yes.'

'Why?'

'Because it is not knowledge. You are wasting yourself on petty questions.'

'And where does being quiet and not asking questions lead you?'

'To that which is beyond question.'

[7] *Ibid.*

50

'Which is?'

'Everything you wish to know... hush now!' I lifted a finger to my lips. 'No more questions!'

We headed towards Bat-Yam.

The silent beach and the waveless, foamless sea which rippled rhythmically probably put Yitschak in a mystical state of mind. We walked past the first sewer pipe where three fishermen were standing, and climbed on the concrete structure over the second sewage pipe. On its left-hand side, there was a slippery wall, about four metres high.

'Who built this wall?' asked Yitschak.

'Probably the municipal council, in order to block the erosion.'

A thorny hillside emerged beyond the wall as we approached a place bearing the English name Sea Place which was translated into Hebrew as: 'Sea Palace'. About twenty metres ahead, the road sloped, merging with the narrow strip of beach. On my left I noticed a glittering patch of reflected rays from the setting sun, bright and alluring.

A vague shadow of the word *greed* reappeared in my mind. I turned my gaze from Yitschak to the sparkling patch and focused on it.

Yitschak turned back and suddenly ran towards the source of the glittering light. He knelt down and picked up a wrist watch with a gold bracelet.

'What luck!' he cried with a sparkle in his eyes. I gave him a shrewd look. His enthusiasm cooled down a little.

'A gold watch!' he said.

'Put that object back in its place.' I smiled at him.

'What!' He stood there bewildered, looking from the watch to me and back again.

'We were just talking about greed...'

'But sir, that would be total foolishness!' he

screamed, not grasping my meaning though noticing my tone of voice.

'It doesn't belong to you,' I continued.

'True, but that's not a good enough reason to put it back in the sand. It could be damaged. Even its owner wouldn't have liked that, and who is he anyway?' Yitschak asked and answered himself with astonishing swiftness, 'He has probably forgotten all about it and if he hasn't he will have presumed it was found by someone else... and if not... how can he possibly find it in the sand? Even if he comes here to look for it he won't be able to find it, I give you my word on that! We are the owners of the watch...' he decided, and then corrected himself when he saw the look in my eyes, 'at the moment...'

'Yitschak,' I said with emphasis, 'you are drugged!'

'Me? With what?'

'With greed.'

He recovered himself and inspected the watch carefully.

'I agree with you,' he said, and added with a sign, 'we will deposit the watch at the police station. If the owner comes and asks for it – it's his. If he doesn't – that's our good luck! That is the law, based on justice and reason!'

'Law, justice and reason are fictions of the illusionary world.'

'But holy books of all kinds praise law, justice and reason...'

'Every written piece of paper belongs to the world of illusion.'

'I don't understand,' commented Yitschak and tightened his grip around the watch, 'The holy books talk also of divinity, the absolute...'

'This is like attempting to learn about the living

52

from the dead. Law, justice, reason and holy books are the absolute without absolute.'

'However,' Yitschak said, returning to our main subject, 'I'm not giving up the watch; you are entitled to give up your share of it!'

'I'm giving you both up!' I said decisively and headed towards the road leading down to the beach. I had gone about a dozen steps when Yitschak reached me, shouting right into my ear, 'All right! I give up! Here, I'm putting the watch back where I found it!'

'I'm not deaf, you know!' I remarked, turning back to him.

He went back and put the watch in the sand.

'A little further,' I said, pointing to the exact place from where he had taken it.

'What difference does it make?' he said, grimacing but picked up the watch and put it back in its rightful place. Then, head down, he walked silently beside me, shrugging his shoulders in a way that was supposed to express wonder and reservation.

We walked down the road and sat down a few metres from it. Before we were comfortably seated, we noticed a man dressed casually in a white short-sleeved flannel shirt and striped shorts. He probably noticed us while advancing in our direction. When he passed by the watch, his eyes were attracted by the same sparkling reflection. He deviated from his path to examine the nature of the phenomenon. As he came closer to the watch which lay in the sand, he seemed to notice it. For a minute or two he stayed put, then cast an inquisitive glance at our direction, knelt down, picked up the watch, straightened up and froze as if considering his next move. His grip tightened carefully around his find.

A blue jeep appeared on the hill, speeding down the road towards the beach.

The man finally reached a decision. He started marching towards us, concealing great strain under the pretence of calmness.

The sharp noise of the approaching car filled the air. I looked at Yitschak. As the young man walked towards us, Yitschak's eyes focused on the man's clenched fist as if spellbound. All of a sudden, the man leaped and started running backwards in a funny way – with his face towards us and his back to the road.

Before we could take in this extraordinary picture, our ears were almost deafened by the sharp scream of the car's brakes, followed by a loud crash like the banging of a girder into a wall.

I could see the blue jeep hitting the man from behind and flinging him a considerable distance. A shining object flew up in the air. A few frightened youngsters jumped out of the blue open car and ran forward. Yitschak ran towards them. They picked up the unconscious wounded man and pushed him into the jeep. The driver reversed the car onto the road and drove fast into town, probably to the nearest hospital.

Yitschak came back with the watch in his hands. He examined its hands, which had stopped and without a word but with amazing accuracy, returned it to its place in the sand.

On the way back, he whispered as though to himself, 'I didn't know you were a wizard!'

'I'm not.'

'It's amazing! I mean, all that happened just now.'

'What is it that amazes you?'

'This coincidence.'

'That was no coincidence; that was a lesson.'

'Please sir, make yourself clear!'

'The forces which take care of you granted you a

valuable lesson; they tried to suck the poisonous greed out of you.'

'There was no need to hurt a man for that.'

'You know very well there was,' I said, emphasizing my last two words, 'but you have nothing to be sorry about; that man's suffering is registered on your account.'

'My account?' Yitschak said, startled. 'Why?' I returned the watch to its place.'

'But carried it in your heart, and furthermore you shot tons of jealousy and destructive hatred towards the man who took it, and as a result of all that you saw what happened,' I said emphatically.

'I didn't mean it! I'm terribly sorry!'

'No use apologizing.'

'What should I do?'

'Prepare yourself for the forthcoming consequences, for you will pay your debt to the last penny.'

'You mean in future lifetimes?'

'My young friend, you are forgetting the fact of your being a spiritual disciple.'

'What about it?'

'You have a very short time indeed to repay your debts.'

'A few years?'

'A few hours, and maybe even less,' I replied calmly.

'I'm terribly sorry! Please help me! I don't want to be run over by a car!' he cried, holding onto my arm with both hands.

I did not respond.

'Please, my gracious, venerable teacher, at least teach me what to do in order to apply balm before the blow!'

'Pray,' I said. 'Try to pray.'

He knelt down on the sand immediately, looked

up and with an excited voice started a confused prayer. The memory of the blow taken by the young man and the sight of him lying unconscious got his imagination all worked up. Later, when we got into the old Peugeot, he drove with remarkable caution.

'If only you always drove like that,' I remarked with a smile.

'If only everyone drove like that,' he replied.

We arrived at his house. I opened the door and got out of the car, intending to say good-bye and walk away. He probably sensed that and, turning the engine off, leaned through the open window and invited, 'Come and have a cup of…'

He meant to say 'a cup of tea' but didn't have the chance to complete his sentence. A car shot out behind him and hit his car. The old Peugeot, the engine still running, jumped forward and smashed into a nearby post.

Yitschak sank into the driver's seat. A few frightened youngsters jumped out of a blue jeep and ran over to him. One of them cried, 'It is not our day today. Only an hour ago we hit someone…'

Yitschak came out of it with minor injuries – a few scratches and bruises on his face, a dislocated hand and foot and a smashed fender on the car. When we met later, he remarked in a tone of explicit doubt, 'Those forces you mentioned – do they really wish me well?'

'They are doing all they can for you to progress. When you wouldn't learn the lesson of greed from me, they came and taught you.'

'Who are these forces?'

'When you are granted the privilege of knowing them, you'll be grateful, but now…'

'What about *now*?'

'You are still a prisoner of the vicious circle.'

He uttered a faint sigh and lowered his head. Then, remembering something, he lifted his eyes and said sarcastically, 'And the praying you recommended, what good did it do?'

'It is the very reason you are now standing on both feet.'

'You mean to say that…'

'Without it, you'd be on crutches.'

13
A children's game

Seasons come and go. The world of illusion takes on and sheds different shapes, forms, shades and colours. Once shrinking and diminishing, crushing totally and disappearing, then emerging as though out of nothing, spreading in all possible directions; all change and promise of change – all an illusion. The privileged one, who has been released from it, regards it as an adult regards the games of children and at moments which seem in their eyes 'glorious', 'magnificent', 'sublime' or 'sad' and 'depressing', moments of triumph or defeat, he cannot help responding with a burst of loud, pure and strong laughter, overflowing with the glorious might of eternity.

14

The assisting forces

Yitschak waited for me at the front gate of my work place and drove me to his home. In his room, he prepared hot potato soup which we drank silently.

'Mr S,' he turned to me and asked, 'what is the nature of those unseen forces you mentioned?' In order to refresh my memory he quoted, 'That when I'm granted the privilege of knowing them I'll be grateful.'

'In essence,' I replied, 'they are nothing but conducted charges of energy, very similar to human beings, only more liberated.'

'What does that mean?'

'It means they are not yet the absolute although their "texture" is closer to that of the absolute. In a certain sense, they are entities more advanced than the human being, and in another sense, less advanced.'

'Explain, if you please!'

'As far as freedom of action is concerned, they are more advanced – they possess the capacity of determination, but as far as their chances of gaining the absolute are concerned, they are less advanced: that is, their chances of attaining the absolute in their present form are zero. Only he who assumes the flesh has a reasonable chance of gaining the absolute.'

'You mentioned that they assist human beings…'

'One way or another, they assist every person who starts on his way towards absolute freedom, and in doing so they increase their own chances of attaining it themselves.'

'How is that?'

'In order for a piece of iron to be magnetized, you need to rub it with a magnet. These forces which help flesh and blood to attain enlightenment, make contact with that enlightenment and when they return to take a flesh body that contact is activated, consciously or subconsciously, and shortens their way.'

'What kind of assistance are they extending to people?'

'Every creature has different capabilities and disabilities. Man is gifted with thought, reason, will and imagination. He believes he is also gifted with determination but that is not true. In the absolute respect he lacks determination. He considers an issue, weighs and analyses the data, draws a conclusion and decides upon an action. The act of decision is called, in common parlance, determination. The distortion is in the terminology. Determination is the ability of execution. It is that far-sighted fortitude which is required for the realization of an idea. *Execution* means perfect performance. Any other performance is pseudo-execution.'

'But people act…,' Yitschak tried to protest.

'They are not capable of putting an idea into effect. In fact, human beings are helpless though they give a different impression… just as the lizard which cannot fly might seem like a bird and sometimes, when climbing the branch of a tall tree, creates the impression that it has flown. The lizard is unable to fly since it lacks the essential organs for it. The human being lacks the essential organs required for a perfect performance. He makes the correct decisions, goes out and performs them, and indeed they will be perfectly performed, but it is not he who has performed them.'

'Please explain,' asked Yitschak.

'You aspire to attaining enlightenment. You have made the right decision – to do whatever is needed to achieve that goal, but up until now you haven't performed a thing. In the case of the dog as well as that of the watch, you did nothing.'

'One does not release oneself from one's inherent instincts in one day,' Yitschak commented and added, 'Nevertheless, I did perform an action – the watch was returned to its place.'

'Indeed, you did calm the "inherent instincts" but the actual performance of putting the watch back in its place was carried out with the assistance of those unseen forces. They activated you. But when you gain enlightenment, you will be the one activating yourself. You will not be able to reach enlightenment without those assisting forces which complete what you've started and by reason of your very nature you cannot complete.'

'Are those forces gifted with determination?'

'Yes, but within a very limited range of action.'

'What is this range of action?'

'Assistance to people on their way to enlightenment.'

'Do you know them personally?'

'We all know them.'

'I don't know them.'

I burst out laughing, 'If you don't, who does?' I said and my laughter grew louder. 'They even left you their mark as a souvenir.' I pointed out to the scar that was left on his cheek as a result of the accident.

Yitschak blinked his eyes with embarrassment,

'Stop laughing now! It's not nice, even though I can feel there is no sting to your laughter.'

'What sting are you referring to?' I asked, pretending to be keyed up and insulted.

'I meant to say... it's not that I'm offended...'

'What a pity!' I said, pretending I was sorry.

'Why a pity?' he asked with surprise.

'My intention was that you would be profoundly insulted.'

'That, I did not expect from you!' replied Yitschak. 'Usually you are hard to understand, but sometimes...' He searched and failed to find the right word, so he gave up and continued, 'Is this the way you are going to guide me towards enlightenment? Where is the pure love and compassion, the benevolence, the fraternity, prudence and wisdom? Where is the sublime brotherhood and the rest of those exalted virtues you are supposed to be teaching me?'

'That's my point.'

'Do you mean that if I were profoundly insulted, I would have gained all these virtues?'

'Don't garble!' I lifted an admonishing finger at him.

'My intention was that you'd be profoundly insulted!' Yitschak quoted with precision.

'Correct,' I agreed.

'Is it essential to be profoundly insulted in order to gain enlightenment?'

'That's not what I said!'

'Good heavens.' Yitschak exclaimed. 'I don't understand a thing any more.'

'Try again,' I suggested.

'I have tried over and over again!'

'Try once more!'

Yitschak sensed my persistence, relaxed and started pondering.

I made myself comfortable in my chair. The sea grew very pale and the first faint star of autumn hung in the steel-blue sky.

'Did you say your intention was to insult me profoundly?' he asked.

I nodded in approval.

'That means,' he said in a whisper, 'that if I had been profoundly insulted, I would be closer to enlightenment…'

'On one condition.'

'Which is?'

'That you could overcome your insult.'

'Shrewd!' Yitschak cried, offended, and after a short inner struggle added, 'And the fact that I didn't even reach the point of insult?' His eyes searched for mine.

'A pain unfelt due to a defective nervous system does not indicate endurance or having overcome that pain.'

'But you have just mentioned that as flesh and blood I lack the capacity of determination, which means that I could not overcome an insult because of my inability.'

'Indeed you could!'

'How?' wondered Yitschak.

'With the aid of the assisting forces.'

'They are not always assisting.'

'You must learn to activate them. For that, you need to develop yourself and, among other things, to develop a willpower worthy of its name.'

After a prolonged silence, during which Yitschak wondered if he should dare introduce more questions and decided to do so, he started positively to bombard me: 'How will I learn to activitate the assisting forces?'

'You will be taught.'

'By whom?'

'By them. Try to understand,' I explained, 'they would like to be activated.'

'Have they already taught me?'

'No, not yet. But when the time comes – they will.'

'How will I know if they are teaching me?'

'By the outcome of your actions. When an idea that you seemed to start carrying out gets carried through by itself, it is an indication that you are learning.'

'That's assistance, not learning.'

'It's both. When you analyze the process of raising the idea, drawing conclusions, reaching the decision of the action and your approach towards carrying it out, you'll find a few surprising points, such as an exceptional state of mind that has accompanied the whole process.'

'What kind of state of mind?'

'Something like a sleeping person who's not asleep. There is a state in which inwardly and outwardly you seem to be asleep, yet you perceive all the signals of the inner and outer environment. You see everything with amazing clarity although not in full light.'

'Can I activitate the assisting forces with the help of this state of mind?'

'Yes.'

'How?'

'Ask them,' I pointed to the space behind him.

'How do you ask them?'

'When the time comes – they will let you know!' I answered with evident satisfaction and stood up.

15

Cock-a-doodle-doo

Yitschak came down to accompany me. We walked awhile in silence. The streets started emptying even though it wasn't late. People were gathering in their homes for dinner with their families. After dinner they would go out for some entertainment or stay at home and watch TV or just go to bed, each according to his habit.

Near the Magen-David-Adom square there was a small crowd: a few men, some elderly women and two or three young couples. The young ladies of the couples were holding on tightly to their companions' arms with a look of terror mixed with childish curiosity in their eyes.

Yitschak and I went closer and through the crowd we saw a tall, broad-shouldered man with a long scarred face, beating up a child covered in rags.

The man looked wild. His long hair, curly and filthy, fell over his unshaven face and shook with every blow he gave the child. He performed his deed with severity and concentration and – most surprisingly – in silence.

The boy crouched down in order to reduce the range of injury and responded only with carefully calculated reactions, so as not to increase the pain or arouse more anger. He was probably on the verge of passing out. The observers followed the spectacle tensely without uttering a sound. They made no attempt to intervene in any way. One of the old ladies, who noticed our arrival, approached us and found it necessary to explain, 'We shouted, begged, tried to speak kindly and dissuade him,' she said, referring to the man who continued beating the child mercilessly, 'but it was all in vain!' She sighed, shrugging her shoulders helplessly. 'There's nothing to be done: he is his father...'

I ignored the questioning gaze Yitschak gave me.

'Let's go.' I said and headed towards the other side of the street.

'How can you!' he said, standing still.

'There's no point in interfering now. The man is tired and the boy doesn't feel a thing any more... it will be over in a minute.'

'I've got to do something!' he murmured as though to himself and his eyes focused on the man administering the beating.

A second later he made his way through the crowd and confronted him.

'Go to hell!' the man growled. Since Yitschak did not obey, he brutally pushed him aside. Yitschak stumbled and fell on his seat. For a minute he sat still on the pavement with a look of astonishment in his eyes. The fall probably caused him a slight concussion and he lost all train of thought. Then, recovering himself, he got up slowly and with his head down approached me.

'Wild beast!' he muttered, referring to the man who pushed him. 'Let's go,' he finally suggested, 'I can't bear to see it any longer!'

The man, who was agitated by Yitschak, suddenly started increasing the frequency and intensity of his blows. The child ceased responding completely. It was obvious that his life was in danger. I crossed the circle of observers and seized the man's broad, muscular shoulders. 'If you please! Be considerate with yourself, for your own sake,' I said to him with a gentle voice that expressed genuine concern. My eyes and body flowed with warmth such as the man had not known since he was a baby, snuggled in his mother's arms. My behaviour was most unexpected by the people around and especially by the aggressor himself. For a moment he softened and let go of the boy. I used this pause to move the child as far away as possible and pushed him, gently but firmly, into the arms of the lady who had explained to us what had been happening, and apparently had been following me all this time, curious to see how things would turn out.

She received the tiny body and immediately started intensive efforts to help him regain consciousness.

'You! Don't interfere!' The man reverted to his aggressive stance. 'It's none of your business,' he exclaimed and frowned again, banishing the last shred of tenderness from his heart.

'Please!' I continued pleading with the same sincere concern for his welfare. 'You are harming your health,' though obviously the main harm was caused to something far more valuable than his health.

I gained more time. From the corner of my eye I noticed the old lady going further away from us with the boy. He was beginning to walk with a clumsy step, like a drunkard or a blind man. But the man seemed to notice it as well.

'Get out of here! Go to hell!' he growled and tried to push me aside forcibly. I remained standing. His next attempt to push me, which failed, made him focus his attention on me. His thick eyebrows rose in astonishment. He couldn't grasp the relation between my lean body and my resistance force.

'Get out of my way!' he roared and grabbed me with his huge, crude hands. He was probably a professional wrestler or a porter – or both. When his third attempt to push me away failed, he let go of me, stepped back and with his fist landed a smashing blow on my cheek. My body tumbled and fell but rose at once to block his path. He hit out again and achieved the very same result – the tumbling body rose again quickly and blocked his way. He lifted his hand for a third blow… the air whistled in my ears but the blow didn't hit its original target. Yitschak, who stood between us all of a sudden, received it instead and fell at my feet.

At that moment the crowd joined the fray and held the frenzied man from all sides. I gave Yitschak a good shake and he opened his eyes.

'Get up!' I commanded. 'Get up quickly!'

He responded instinctively. His heavy body rose slowly, as though he was drunk or in a dream. We used the turmoil around us to escape to a side street.

The beaten boy was sitting at the street corner and weeping bitterly. The old lady was nowhere to be seen.

'Where do you live?' I asked the boy.

He dried his tears, wiped his nose with his palm and told us where his house was. He was about ten or eleven years old but due to his low stature, his thin body and his badly fitting clothes, he seemed much younger, yet his face was that of an old man and so were his long wet fingers.

'Why does he beat you up?' Yitschak asked.

The boy shrugged his shoulders which were covered in a man's shabby shirt and a sweater that came down to his knees.

'Don't know,' he said. 'He always beats me, wherever and whenever he sees me.'

'Is he your father?'

'Yes, he is my father,' he replied, nodding his large head that hung from a thin childish neck.

'Do you live together?'

'No, I live with my mother, but soon I'll be taken to the children's home. Then it will be better.' He grasped my hand and the three of us made our way to his home. We arrived at a dilapidated house. In one of its corners a young prostitute had taken up residence. she received us reluctantly, since a client was sitting in the corner, waiting for his turn.

'Yosy,' she said, 'it's you... Tomorrow you'll be off my back at last. Mrs Yona is taking you to the children's home!'

'Who is Mrs Yona?' I asked her.

'The social worker... anyway what's with you two... are you interested? I'm cheap.'

We went out into the open air.

'Mr S, won't you come to my place for another cup of tea?' asked Yitschak. I felt it was important for him so I gave my consent. We walked the rest of the way in silence.

We went up to Yitschak's room, where he put the kettle on. A few minutes later, large cups, filled with the hot fragrant liquid were placed on the table facing the open porch. We drank unhurriedly.

'There are two things I don't quite understand.' Yitschak broke the silence. 'The reason why you didn't interfere in the quarrel immediately and the reason why the man couldn't move you.'

I took another tiny sip of the hot liquid and, inspecting the cracks in the upper part of the wall, replied, 'I did not interfere in the quarrel – neither in the beginning nor at the end.'

'Then who took all the blows?'

'You and I.'

'Without interfering in the quarrel?'

'Without interfering in the quarrel.'

'So what were you doing all that time?'

'I was observing the stars.'

'And in the course of doing that you were beaten up, thrown to the ground, rose up and collapsed again!'

'My young friend,' I stopped inspecting the cracks in the wall and turned gently to Yitschak, 'I was observing the stars and something else got beaten up and fell down.'

He pondered over my reply for a long while and finally said, 'You did not answer my question.'

'Which one?'

'Why when we noticed that disgraceful scene you intended to continue on your way, while I was the one who tried to save the poor boy from the paws of that wild beast?'

I watched his tense and serious face. My reply was important to him. 'If you saw a prostitute ordering her pimps to beat up a client in order to rob him… you see, the client had already paid her but she smelled cash and ordered her pimps to beat him severely in order to pick him clean… and later, on another occasion, this client returns to take his revenge on that prostitute by dealing her the very same blows he had received from her pimps… would you interfere on behalf of the prostitute?'

'No,' Yitschak answered without hesitation.

'Imagine,' I said, 'that the boy was once a prostitute and that the "wild beast" was the robbed and beaten client.'

Yitschak stood up and asked with awe and reverence, 'Are you clairvoyant?'

I joined my palms to my mouth in the shape of a funnel, open towards the outside and cried out loud: 'Cock-a-doodle-doo!'

Yitschak was alarmed at first but recovered and tried to insist, 'You are clairvoyant Mr S, aren't you?'

'Cock-a-doodle-doo!' I cried. The imitation was perfect, and the proof was that an elderly lady from the opposite building hurried to open her window in a desperate attempt to locate the crowing cock along the narrow, damp and dingy street.

Yitschak gave up. After a few minutes of silence he changed the subject and asked, 'And what about the merciful justice which ensures spiritual progress?'

'To whom?'

'To whomever,' he said, confused.

'Indeed, you are right, mercy for all! For the former prostitute and her cheated client – the "wild beast" of today. And that is exactly what I did.'

'But why did you wait?' insisted Yitschak.

I lowered my head and examined the tiled floor for a long time. It looked quite filthy in the lamp's strong light. Then I said, 'Firstly, because the scene was about to end if you hadn't interferred, and secondly, do you know the story of the three yogis?'

'Which yogis?'

'Those who hung their garments in the air.'

'No, I don't know it. Please tell me!'

'Three yogis bathed in the holy Ganges. They washed their garments in it and hung them in the air to dry.

Suddenly they noticed, high in the sky, an eagle preying on a pigeon. The first one turned to the eagle and said, "Let go of it!" His garment dropped to the ground. The second one, too, spoke to the eagle. "Eat it," he said, "it is your nature!" His garment fell to the ground as well. The third one sat silently and did not

71

interfere. His garment stayed hanging in the air, drying in the joyful sun.'

'But you did interfere!' remarked Yitschak.

'It was not an interference,' I answered.

'Then what was it?'

'Nothing.'

Yitschak pondered for quite a while and was probably trying to phrase a question which would force me to clarify what required clarification, in a way that he could understand. When he finally managed to do so he asked, 'What is an interference?'

'An action involving the "I".'

'And an action which does not involve the "I" – is it not interference?'

'An action which does not involve the "I" is not an action at all.'

'What is an action?'

'A deed which produces results.'

'A deed in which the "I" is not involved does not produce results?'

'Neither in present nor in future.'

'If a man commits murder without involving the "I" in the act, will he not bear the consequences?'

'No, he will not bear the consequences.'

'How is it possible to be released of the "I" while in action?'

'It's impossible.'

'Why?'

'Either you are totally free of the "I", when in action as well as when not, or you are not released of it when in action and when not in action.'

'Who is free of the "I"?'

'The enlightened.'

'Are you free of the "I"?' he asked, trying in vain to seize this opportunity to extract a statement from me.

'The enlightened is free of the "I".'

He sighed in despair and changed the subject by reminding me, 'I asked another question.'

'About my confrontation with the man.'

'That's right.'

'It's a matter of expressing your will,' I answered.

'Is it enough to express my will in order to resist a power twice as strong as mine successfully?'

'Yes.'

'And if I want to fly?'

'You will fly.'

'I want to fly, right this minute!' cried Yitschak and stayed stuck to his chair. 'Where are the results?' he asked, disappointed.

'Your will is not realized because it does not exist,' I explained. 'You have no will.'

'What is a will?'

'A wish which materializes when expressed.'

'Only the enlightened possesses a will?' sneered Yitschak.

'Not everyone who has achieved enlightenment also possesses a will.'

'Then who possesses a will?'

'Sorcerers of all kinds and enlightened people who wish to possess it.'

'Why don't all the enlightened wish to possess will?'

'Because there is a certain danger in their becoming will-possessing. One might get recaptured in the vicious circle of the illusionary world because the will exists in the world of illusion and belongs to it.'

'Even the enlightened might get recaptured in the vicious circle of the illusory world?'

'Theoretically – yes. In actual fact – no.'

'How is that?'

'Is it possible to recover and remake chains that

were broken, melted down and vanished from the face of the earth?'

'Yes, it's possible,' said Yitschak.

'Theoretically, but not practically.'

'And what of the sorcerers?' Yitschak did not forget to ask.

'They are an inseparable part of the circle.'

I stood up.

'Can I drive you home?' he offered.

'I'd be grateful,' I said. A glance at my watch made me realize it was already 1 am and the bus service has stopped long ago.

16

The beginning
of awareness
as a feeling of relief

I arrived at Yitschak's place at nightfall. At his request, we had started meeting once a week on Mondays. Yitschak was working as a technician for a company that manufactured electronic instruments. Monday was their 'easy' day – a day of preparation.

He welcomed me with a bright face and just as I sat down he flung at me a sentence which had become habitual, 'I have lots of questions!'

He was about to bring the fruit tray when I stopped him.

'Just a minute,' I said. 'Please sit down!'

'Right away,' he said, not understanding my meaning. 'I'll just go and get the fruit…'

'Sit down please!' I stressed. He returned reluctantly and sat down at the other side of the table.

'From now on, we will open every meeting with half an hour of silence, in which you can repeat your mantra.'

'What for?' he asked, disconcerted.

'Questions at the end!' I smiled at him. I straightened the upper part of my body and disconnected from S.

I am myself, as I have always been and eternally will be. There are no words to express that. If there were any I would be bound to them in some way, whereas what I truly am is absolute freedom, which is the utter reverse of any tie.

I am infinity, goodness and immortality, eternal happiness, pure love and the sincere aspiration for them. This aspiration is the fundamental principle of existence, the source of absolute faith, and the basis of the hope which leads to me. When this hope has lost its sincerity, it deforms into petty, capricious desires, shady lusts and enslaving wishes.

Lacking in clear thinking, people try to satisfy their wishes, desires and lusts in the world of illusion, and suffer disappointments, disillusionment and despair. Eventually, these disappointments and disillusionments turn their attention from the trivial goals they tried to achieve in the illusory world, to me that live eternally within them – the sole purpose of their life. Through the years, generations and eras they change and grow more and more aware of me. In a way, this awareness induces a feeling of relief, like the feeling of a man who is plunged into a nightmare and yet knows it is only a nightmare.

17

More than mere answers

Half an hour went by. I turned to Yitschak. 'The questions!' I reminded him.

'There aren't any,' he replied. 'No questions.'

'You've forgotten them?'

'Not exactly.'

'You found the answers?'

'No.'

'Then why don't you ask them?'

'They…' Yitschak pondered, 'they reduced, revoked themselves, became unnecessary. It's not that they were answered but they don't seem like questions any more.' He gave me an inquisitive look which I ignored, and he then felt obliged to ask, 'What happened here?'

'We disregarded language as an explanatory means and gained an explanation.'

'Not exactly,' Yitschak tried to feign objection. 'It's not as though you supplied me with answers… In fact…' he pondered again, 'there are more than mere answers here. The nature of answers is to bring forth new questions and so on…'

'And there is no end to it,' I remarked.

'And in this case?' his eyes enquired again.

'You can't rid yourself of this bad habit of yours!'

'Which one?'

'To prattle. You have transcended a few words and immediately you pile up new ones.'

'I'm about to propose...' opened Yitschak solemnly.

'An additional silence?"

'You guessed!'

'The proposition is accepted.'

Again, I disconnected from S, returning to my true nature as perfect happiness, endless peacefulness, pure love and all the rest of these shallow words which are absolutely incapable of describing me, for how could the light be described to those born blind?

Lacking explosives, one tries to remove a mountain with one's bare hands. The result? The mountain disappears voluntarily.

The additional half-hour passed. Yitschak gave me a radiant look. 'I'm happy with the way you chose to answer me!' he said and let his eyes float over the enormous space of the greyish sea. 'Nevertheless,' he added, 'a tiny little question still bothers me – what function does language serve on the way to fulfilment?'

'This time, we don't need any silences,' I replied, 'In the absolute sense, language is an obstacle. It is unable to describe the tiniest little fraction of the truth, despite its pretension to do so. People who are attached to language are left with the choice between total distortion of the truth or minimal distortion.'

'But language has noble sources,' Yitschak remarked hesitatingly.

'All of man's earthly desires are a frightful distortion of his yearning for freedom. Language was created as a response to those aberrant desires. Its purpose is to chain people to one another with a tight linguistic bond. Indeed, it also has a positive purpose as far as the spiritual disciple is concerned.'

'Which is?'

'Metaphorically speaking, you can say that language is a baby's dummy, designed to still his craving for his mother's milk, from which he was weaned, and make his way to the adult's solid food less painful. The "dummy" serves as a means of softening the transitional period of his development.'

'If so,' replied Yitschak, 'whoever attains enlightenment becomes utterly silent!'

'Towards himself – yes. As to others who need his guidance – no. To them, he is like a mother who sticks a dummy in her weeping baby's mouth.'

'I'm going to bring the fruit,' announced Yitschak and disappeared into his little kitchen. He returned with the famous Chinese plate, filled with grapes and a few dates.

'This is a most valuable plate,' I remarked as I took a tiny cluster of grapes.

'It's valuable twice over to me,' answered Yitschak as he sat down. He explained, 'It's valuable because of its market price and also because it's a memento of that famous geologist, my great-grandfather, who lived in China for some time.'

The grapes were sweet but not as sweet as the big honey-shaded dates.

'Silence, then, is the best way of imparting spiritual knowledge,' Yitschak tried to resume.

'There is no other way,' I said.

'Do you mean that until today we haven't dealt with any attempt to approach enlightenment at all?' he asked.

'Yes we have, in the same way as a man who intends to go on a long and arduous journey prepares his provision, polishes his equipment, throws a farewell party for his friends, etc.'

'And as of today are we on our way?'

'I did not say that.'

'You stated that our situation is similar to someone who prepares his provisions, etc.'

'That's right. The preparation is considered part of starting out.'

'Mr S, if you please, explain to me, little by little.' He lowered his voice and yet made it sound clear, 'When you said that there is no other way leading to the absolute except silence, what did you mean?'

'What I said.'

'That is, that until today we were dealing with preparations only?'

'Not only preparations,' I said, increasing his bewilderment.

'With what else?'

'With a trial. Before anyone embarks on a journey – and we are talking about a long and hard one – he must be examined and tested in order to see if he can endure its hardships. That's what we've been doing until today. That is also what we are doing now and will be doing in the next few days.'

'And what about the silence?'

'It's the only way that leads to the absolute.'

'But we have been dealing with silence today.'

'We were testing ourselves,' I corrected and emphasized, 'We've been testing ourselves!'

'But a moment ago you agreed that we have indeed been dealing with "an attempt to approach enlightenment!"' he quoted himself with precision of which I approved very much.

'That's right,' I nodded in agreement.

'And now you are saying something else.'

'Not at all. We were dealing with an *attempt*,' I said, with emphasis on the word "attempt". 'That means, we were inspecting and analyzing the special

80

conditions of the road before marching onto it.'

'In what way is silence superior to all the rest of the ways?' Yitschak changed the subject, withholding a sigh.

'All the other ways create a connection. Take language for instance – with its assistance, a connection is created between groups of people. He who goes out on the road to achieving enlightenment must free himself of any connection or attachment whatsoever, or more precisely, he must aspire to freedom from any connection or attachment whatsoever.'

'Why did you change "must" into "must aspire"?'

'Anyone who has not yet gained enlightenment is incapable of breaking off any connection or attachment and vice versa – the enlightened has cut off all his attachments and connections, and therefore is enlightened. The spiritual disciple who aspires to enlightenment is actually aspiring to being released of all his connections and attachments.'

'How will the unenlightened become enlightened if he is incapable of breaking off any connection or attachment, but can only aspire to that?'

'His sincere aspiration calls in the assisting forces and with their help enlightenment is achieved.'

'Isn't silence an attachment?'

'The perfect silence is in fact the absolute freedom and only the enlightened grasp it. Relative silence has a certain power since it is a reflection of the perfect silence. This power strengthens the disciple's yearning for the absolute. It stops the connections and attachments from tightening their grip around his neck.'

'Does silence prevent the connections and attachments from tightening their grip?'

'Yes.'

'But the connections and attachments remain connections and attachments!'

'Certainly. And should the spiritual disciple let go of the silence, they will drag him down to hell.'

'We haven't exercised silence up until today.'

'That's not true,' I remarked. 'Contemplation is also silence. Don't ever let go of it!'

18

The attachments,
grief and anger: a trial

The grapes were almost finished. The sky was strewn with bright stars. Yitschak got up and put on the light in the room.

'To be honest,' he remarked, returning to his chair, 'I don't feel any attachment to anything, not even to my parents. I'm hardly attached to anything. Maybe to you a little, but that's like an attachment to freedom.'

'You are tightly attached to all of the illusory world, not with strings but with thick and heavy ropes!' I replied laughing.

'I beg your pardon! That's not true,' he said offended.

'It's the naked truth,' I insisted. 'A relative truth as well as an absolute truth, whichever kind of truth you like.'

'This is just annoying talk.'

'Here, you've just admitted to being attached to anger.'

'I didn't say that,' he said defensively. 'What you are saying is annoying but not to me! I haven't known any grief or anger for quite some time now and despite your remarks you could say I've advanced by quite a few meaningful steps.'

'No grief and no anger?' I asked him calmly.

'No grief and no anger,' he replied with a deep voice as if looking into his heart, drawing conclusions and publicizing them.

On the famous Chinese plate there were still a few dates and a single abandoned cluster of grapes. I transferred them carefully to the table, which was covered with a white nylon table cloth. Then, I picked up the plate with both hands, lifted it to the level of my shoulders, noticing the little hanger affixed to its side while doing so, and threw it forcibly onto the tiled floor. The antique Chinese porcelain smashed into many uneven pieces which scattered instantly all over the room.

Yitschak was paralysed. He bent over towards me with his mouth wide open. His eyes were wandering through the air, refusing to look down onto the floor, and his face was ashen.

'Ha ha ha ha,' I laughed loudly and my laughter grew louder and louder. 'Ha ha ha,' I went on laughing. 'No grief and no anger,' I teased him, distorting the tone of his voice into a weeping tone and went on laughing without stopping.

Yitschak blushed, recovered himself and all of a sudden screamed, 'Enough, damn it, enough!' But I continued to laugh even more loudly than before.

Suddenly he crouched down in his chair as if seized by a convulsion and started weeping like a baby.

'Have we gone far!' I shouted, making no attempt to hold back my laughter. He tried to overcome his weeping but couldn't; his shoulders continued shaking. He hid his face with the palms of his hands.

'Would you want me to collect all the broken pieces and reassemble the plate by sticking them together? There are all kinds of glues these days, you know!' I suggested, trying to moderate my laughter.

Since there was no response I went down on my knees and started collecting the pieces one by one, piling them up on the table. I sat down and then calmly and very seriously started to join the pieces back together again.

While doing so I was singing as though to myself:

I wish Yitschak stopped crying
over his favourite plate.
That's why I'm really trying
to mend its broken fate.

And indeed Yitschak was no longer weeping. He looked at me with wide-open eyes that expressed immeasurable bewilderment.

'Who are you, Mr S?' he asked me with a piercing voice.

'A smashed Chinese plate,' I answered.

19

Fear! But do not sink into complacency

I do not know if Yitschak will awaken and reach me in his present lifetime. Indeed, he is putting in a lot of effort, but that's not enough. On the way to eternity, as well as in mortal life, you need a touch of luck, a combination of circumstances and a co-ordination of events which bring about the one-time 'great clash' and release a man from his ancient prison of passions and desires.

After half an hour of silence, I revealed to Yitschak, 'Soon you will reach the end of the trial period.'

'Does that mean I need to prepare for that battle you described in the beginning of our acquaintance-ship?'

'We've always been preparing for it.'

'But there are no results.'

'Yes, there are.'

'Even in the case of the plate I did not pass the test.'

'You are incapable of passing it,' I said and added, 'You must understand once and for all that you are incapable of passing a test. You lack the qualifications for that and will continue to lack them until the appointed time of the "great clash". In the meantime you are accumulating power which you will need at that fateful hour.'

'What is that power needed for at that fateful hour that, as far as I understand, comes about by itself?'

'First, this power growing and accumulating inside you attracts the hour of decision in the same way that a growing electrical charge attracts more intensely its opposite electrical charge. Secondly, at the time of the fateful event your power will assist you not to miss it.'

'Please be more specific,' demanded Yitschak.

'If the man, for whom the one-time fateful event occurs and who in fact has appointed it for himself, is not ready for it, it will pass over him without his noticing it. That means he will return to the illusory world for an immeasurable number of years.'

'Does that mean that a man who has not accumulated power might miss his one and only chance of a lifetime?'

'Definitely,' I stated. 'But it doesn't work that way. As I already told you – man is in fact the main cause of the "great clash"; he brings it into the world. His faith, exercises and yearnings are always aimed at it alone.'

'In what way is this accumulated power expressed?'

'In constant alertness towards that very event. A touch of luck, of course, is also needed, as well as a co-ordination of circumstances and what is called – coincidence.'

'I'm beginning to fear,' remarked Yitschak.

'It's better to fear than to sink into complacency. Anyway, cases of a miss are almost unknown. That doesn't mean they have not occurred, but because of the very essence of their nature they do not become known.'

'Not clear,' announced Yitschak.

'Those who have missed are obviously people

incapable of being aware of their miss. They return to the world of appearances with the conviction that they must continue to exercise in order to gain fulfilment. You can meet such people in remote monasteries in Tibet, India, China and in the snowy Pyrenean mountains or in the Peninsula of Athos in Greece.'

'We must do everything to prevent myself from reaching that state,' demanded Yitschak.

'We are doing everything, but not everything is in our hands. As I mentioned, there is a very tiny part – a tenth of a percent – which is not dependent upon us but nevertheless has the power to ruin everything.'

'Mr S, I can't understand how my unsuccessful exercises could advance me or, more precisely, cause the accumulation of power within me.'

'I've explained to you before, every exercise causes changes in thought, will and sensibility. At first a slight and delicate change but in time – considerable and meaningful. You don't sense these changes because of their primary subtlety and because of the habit involved. A baby does not sense his growing up; he receives food and grows. These changes are power, a growing charge of energy. The substantial expression of this energy is vigilance, external as well as internal. It is vigilance of every detail and every movement, constant alertness and peaceful preparedness towards the approaching great event. The more vigilant the spiritual disciple is, the closer is the hour of decision.'

'How is that?' Yitschak asked.

'This accumulated power,' I clarified, 'in consequence to the effort invested in the exercises, attracts the hour of decision and eventually brings it into the world.'

'To this world?'

'To the world,' I said without explaining. He did

not press me; instead he asked: 'In what way is that vigilance expressed.'

'It's possible to define it as excessive precision in giving details, or in more acceptable but inaccurate words, as a growing attachment to the truth.'

'The second definition is closer to my heart.'

'It is more acceptable, but transgresses against the truth.'

'Please clarify this statement.'

'A man whose vigilance is growing transfers faithfully what he has received. Not in general terms but word for word. He also pays attention to the frequently changing meaning of what has been said.'

'Please give an example,' asked Yitschak.

'Not long ago we talked about engaging in trials on the way to enlightenment, the same week that the connection between you and that antique Chinese plate was broken.'

'I remember,' Yitschak grimaced as if trying to rid himself of an unpleasant memory.

'Then you quoted me accurately but without grasping the meaning of it: "We were dealing with an attempt to approach enlightenment." You did not pay attention to the word "attempt" and to its crucial meaning. You interpreted the sentence as if we were dealing directly with an approach to enlightenment and not with an *attempt* to approach enlightenment.'

'Then too, you have corrected my inaccuracy.'

'True.'

Yitschak remained silent for a while, then held his head up and as a wide smile spread all over his face he said, 'Now your method is clear to me!'

'What method?' I said surprised.

'To fool me and keep on fooling me and in this way to arouse my attention to the small details!'

'God forbid! It didn't even occur to me to try and

89

fool you; all I've done was to clarify that which needed clarification in the most clear and beneficial way.'

'Mr S, I'm most deeply grateful to you!'

'Don't be foolish!'

'What do you mean?' he asked tensely, since he had learned to recognize the power of a hidden meaning lying behind every sentence, accidental as it might appear.

'Have you ever heard of a man who thanks himself or, as you said, "is grateful" to himself?'

'But it was you I meant,' he clarified, anticipating my reply.

'That's what I said,' I emphasized. 'It is foolish to be "grateful" to yourself!'

'Mr S,' Yitschak almost despaired, 'I was referring to you. I was expressing my thanks to you. Don't you understand what I'm saying?'

'That's what I said,' I repeated. 'You are trying to express your thanks to yourself and there's no greater foolishness!'

I stood up, implying that the conversation had ended.

20

Truth, illusion, lie

Winter was in the air. The cold was accumulating in the corners of Yitschak's room. We stopped sitting on the terrace, closed its multi-shuttered sliding windows and sat not far from it.

After the half-hour of silence Yitschak said, 'In our last meeting we vaguely touched on the "increasing attachment to the truth" concerning the advanced spiritual disciple. Could you clarify this?'

'The truth is a complex matter. In fact, there is but one truth – the absolute truth. Hence the lie, by its very nature, does not exist. With a little bit of word play and a dust of philosophy, what comes out is that whatever we see, breathe, feel and hear is nothing but truth.'

'Or maybe doesn't exist,' remarked Yitschak.

'Then how could we hear it, see it, breathe it and feel it?' I contradicted. He was confused and went silent.

'My point is,' I went on, 'that all we breathe, see, etc., is not what we perceived in a certain unit of time because by the time we have absorbed it, it has already changed. What we perceived is different from its origin. We do not absorb the origin. The lie does not exist and so is the thing which was absorbed by our senses. It no longer exists by the time we absorb it. Furthermore, the absorbing organs are not the same. With every passing unit of time they too change. This causes embarrassment since we are accustomed to thinking that we are absorbing true pictures with our eyes, true sounds with our ears and true sensations with our skin. All of this doesn't withstand the most superficial test. Nevertheless, it is not a lie but...'

'But what?' urged Yitschak.

'An illusion,' I replied.

Yitschak tried to examine me closely and when he did not succeed he asked, 'What is the difference between a lie and an *illusion*?'

'A *lie* is the opposite of truth. An *illusion* is a derivative of the truth.'

'In other words, illusion is a certain kind of truth,' he said.

'A *certain kind of truth* does not exist; either the truth is one or it is not truth.'

'What is then an illusion?'

'I have just said...'

'A derivative of the truth?'

'A sort of a secretion, something like sweat.'

'I don't understand,' admitted Yitschak.

'A body secretes sweat. The body's sweat is not the body itself but you might say it belongs to it because it is secreting it. The sweat doesn't interest the body at all; all the same, it has a certain connection with it. The body is not sweat just as the sweat is not the body. This is the correct distinction and whoever grasps this distinction can distinguish between truth and illusion.'

'And the lie?'

'The lie has nothing to do with this. You don't distinguish the nonexistent.'

'Can one distinguish the illusion?'

'Yes – as an illusion. Naturally, there is also a mistaken distinction – when the one who is making it is himself a part of the illusion. A man who identifies himself with his body, which is an inseparable part of the illusion, is liable to claim that this body is real and that the spirit is a figment of the imagination.'

'Is this distinction vital?'

'At a certain stage of evolution – as vital as air.'

'At which stage.'

'At the immediate stage after achieving enlightenment. Later on there is no need for it. It is annulled by itself. The enlightened one, who has awakened to knowing himself as an inseparable part of the eternal infinity, does not sense and obviously does not pay any attention to the natural illusion which is inspired by him. Its objective in any case is extinction.'

'What does it mean, "The advanced disciple should be attached to the truth"?' Yitschak repeated.

'To try and deliver things as they are, after making the effort to receive them as they are. It's not that he can't be caught up in a lie. The lie in the kingdom of illusion is not defined as a lie. Most people are lying without being aware of it. In fact, it's impossible for a man of flesh and blood not to lie.'

'*Is that so?*' Yitschak emphasized, attempting to contradict me.

I tried to explain, 'When you tell someone that the time is *twenty minutes past seven*, you are relying on your watch, which like any other watch in the world is not absolutely precise. Any measuring, including the measuring of time, is conditioned, that is, a lie. Nevertheless, all mankind is tightly attached to this lie. When you announce that the time is *twenty minutes past seven* you are lying. But if you add to it "according to my watch", you will break the frame of conventions and become closer to the truth with a tiny step. This will cause a change in your personality – an advancing change as far as your yearning for fulfilment is concerned. On the other hand, you will seem strange in people's eyes.'

'In what way will this be expressed?'

'If you are consistent in this, an invisible but very real "excommunication" will surround you. If, for the sake of your purpose, you ignore the invisible ban, then you will gain an additional positive change in your personality or, in other words, you will continue to accumulate power. If you continue to increase your devotion to the relative truth and will not "round off" the time but deliver it precisely – to yourself, as well as to others who ask you: "The time is seven and eighteen and a half minutes "according to my watch" – you will gain an additional progress.'

'Progress towards the destined hour,' he said, trying to let me know that he was following my speech and understood my meaning.

'The power is indeed directed at the great event and is also directing you towards it; furthermore, it is in itself a charge of energy in the conventional sense of the word. It is a charge of energy which is very easy to detect.'

'How could it be detected in the case of giving the most precise time?'

'If you are consistent in delivering the most accurate time possible according to your watch, to yourself as well as to others, you will soon find out that your watch has become the most accurate watch in the city, and probably in the whole country.'

'How soon would that happen?'

'Between one and three years.'

'Mr S, I'm going to try that.'

'Try and you will see.'

'And what if I am devoted to the relative truth in other fields as well.'

'Then your power will spread and increase to such

94

an extent that whatever seems true to you will eventually become true.' In order to give an answer before the question, I added, 'If a sick man seems healthy to you, he will recover right there and then.'

'We've raised this subject in one of our first conversations,' Yitschak pointed out.

'That's right,' I agreed, 'but we did not discuss this new way of control over energies in that conversation.'

'Which way?'

'Attachment to the truth. This attachment obviously requires the utmost vigilance. Vigilance of conception as well as delivery. Knowing that at this minute you are sitting with your right hand on the table and your left on the back support of the chair while your eyes observe the yellow wall and your ears absorb the rhythmic sound of the sea, without letting any incidental thought or bursting emotion disturb you – is vigilance of absorption. To deliver the facts alone, without adding even a little bit of your own thoughts or emotions – is the vigilance of transmission. If you are vigilant twenty-four hours a day, you will quickly reach your zero hour and also control the energies and be able to do with them whatever you please.'

'Why doesn't the enlightened do with the energies "whatever he pleases"?'

'You've already asked a similar question. The enlightened does not "please" anything. He clearly sees there is nothing real about the energies. Would an adult try to gratify his hunger with a baby's dummy instead of a delicious meal?'

'If the dummy is the energies, what is the delicious meal?'

'Enlightenment.'

95

21

A proper reading
of an appropriate book

We continued to sit silently in the dim room even when the half hour of silence had passed. Yitschak moved in his seat. I asked him to put on the light.

'Do you read books?' I asked.

'Before your translations fell into my hands, I used to devour all kinds of books, I mean creative literature of all kinds. But afterwards they lost their charm as far as I was concerned.'

'You don't read books any more?'

'Creative literature I seldom read, but books of philosophy and wisdom I read constantly.'

'Very good,' I said. 'Books may cause most favourable changes within us, for the accumulation of positive power.'

'Vigilance?'

'Vigilance.'

'Any book whatsoever?'

'The best of them. One should cultivate proper reading in an appropriate book.'

Yitschak pointed towards a long shelf on the wall which was stacked with books. 'The crème de la crème!' he said with a touch of pride in his voice.

'An appropriate book is not enough,' I remarked. 'One must also cultivate proper reading.'

'What is proper reading?'

'Reading which brings about advancing changes. Today we will dedicate our time to proper reading in the appropriate book.' I pointed to a book which lay on the tiny table under the shelf and asked him, 'Hand me that book.'

Yitschak stood up with the obvious intention of carrying out my request. Halfway across the room he stopped, pondered for a moment and finally turned to me and asked softly, 'Which book did you mean?'

'The crème de la crème,' I imitated him, still pointing to the book on the tiny table, underneath the shelf.

Yitschak did not move. 'I apologize for repeating the question,' he said, 'but what do you regard as "the cream of the cream"?'

'It is not a repeated question,' I remarked. 'First, you asked about proper reading.'

'True,' he said apologetically.

'A good book is a book that, when read properly, creates progressive changes. An unfit book is a book that inhibits development.'

'What is creative literature in your eyes?'

'An unfit book,' I replied without any hesitation. 'It cultivates the worship of temporary sensual pleasures. The source of creative literature are the senses. Its path – senses. And its end – the glorifying of them; that is to say, the glorification of the enslavement. Even the bits of "truth" scattered in it here and there are saturated with the mortality of the senses.'

'But there is also a different kind of creative literature,' Yitschak dared to remark.

'There is creative literature without creative literature.'

'Please explain!'

'There is literature that despite its readability and acceptability to the senses, is not the result of fusion of senses. Its aim is inculcating mastery over the senses.'

'For example?'

'This literature we are creating at this moment, the dialogue between us. The one who aspires to self-mastery will read it and benefit from it. Please be good enough to bring me the book I asked for.' I pointed again to the thick book.

Yitschak did not move.

'Mr S,' he said, 'I think you are making a mistake.'

'I'm not making a mistake.'

'If you are referring to the great thick book that's on the table, underneath the shelf, I'm sure you are making a mistake!'

'I'm not making a mistake,' I said conclusively. He turned his whole body towards me with emphasis, as if trying by that impressive movement to prove to me that I was mistaken. Then, articulating his words and with exaggerated clarity, he informed me solemnly, 'The book you are asking for is none other then the phone book.' He even tried to demonstrate a restrained giggle.

'I'm not short-sighted,' I replied. 'That's the book I was referring to.'

'The phone book?' Yitschak refused to believe his ears.

'That's the one.'

The familiar thick book was placed in front of me.

'Sit down please,' I invited Yitschak to sit next to me so that we could both read it at the same time.

'Do you mean to say that the phone book is "the wisest of books"?' Yitschak murmured, unable to overcome his disbelief.

'The very wisest of the wise!!!'

'And reading it…'

'The proper reading of it,' I stressed, 'is the kind of reading which creates progressive changes and brings about the accumulation of power and the formation of strong vigilance.'

'I wish I could believe that.'

'And so you shall,' I stressed and commanded, 'read!'

'Where should I start?'

'At the beginning. Well, read!'

He turned over the front page but I stopped him.

'From the beginning, we said.'

'Where is the beginning?'

'The front page.'

Yitschak leaned over and started reading reluctantly, 'The Telephone Directory,' then, as he was about to turn over the page, I stopped him by placing my hand on the book.

'This is not proper reading,' I remarked.

He stared at me in astonishment. 'And what is proper reading?'

'A full and complete reading. You haven't read even one line properly.'

'Aha,' he uttered with a smile, 'I forgot the foreign[8] year number – 1974.'

He attempted to turn the thick front page but I was compelled to stop him again. 'When you make a mistake, you go back to the very beginning.'

'What do you mean?'

'Start from "The Telephone Directory", etc.'

Yitschak sighed but obeyed and read, 'The Telephone Directory 1974.' His swift fingers slid across

---

[8] Jews have a different count of years. It is written in Hebrew letters which have a numerical value.

the front page with an apparent intention of turning it over. Once again, I prevented him from doing so. 'Man!' I cried, 'you don't know how to read at all. You can't perform even a simple reading, let alone proper reading!'

Yitschak was utterly confused.

'But I've read everything,' he protested vehemently.

'That's a lie!' I leant towards him and continued, 'Read everything! And from the very beginning please.'

He tried several times. At one point he left out the 'Tel-Aviv dialling area code' and another time the digits 03 appearing on that line or the number of the foreign year. Every omission brought him back to the very beginning. By the eighth time he managed to read all the printed signs which appeared on the front page.

'That's proper reading,' I declared. 'Go on!'

Yitschak turned the front page carefully and started reading the advertisement of the Post Office Bank printed on the inside. He made more than a few mistakes and each one brought him back to the front page. There were also times when he repeatedly left out one of the prefix digits...

After an hour of 'proper reading' he managed to get to the third page of the telephone directory which was 'Applications to the Engineering Services'. I stopped him there and said, 'We will leave that for our next meeting.'

'So this is the "proper reading",' he grumbled, his face still tense. A few seconds later, he relaxed and a wide smile spread over his face.

'*Proper reading* indeed,' he sighed with relief and added, 'I've learnt the Standing Order of the Post Office Bank by heart...'

'Excuse me,' I interrupted, 'it's not *The* Standing Order, but just "Standing Order" without the definite article – Standing Order of the Post Office Bank.'

'Yes, yes,' he agreed hastily in fear of having to read again from this horrendous book.

'What is the point of this kind of reading?' he cried. 'It can only make any desire for reading hateful!'

'Or suppress any hatred whatsoever,' I answered.

'How?'

'By the cultivation of true patience. Reading readable books in which the story drugs the reader and enslaves him to some ephemeral hero who cannot tell his right foot from his left is nothing but stupefying reading. *Proper reading* on the other hand, is reading which creates advancing changes. It is not easy and in order to win the great prize you need to put your whole heart and soul into constant effort…'

'…And must read the most boring books!' said Yitschak.

'Must exercise *proper reading* in the wisest books,' I corrected him.

'Like this one,' Yitschak sneered and pointed at 'The Telephone Directory 1974 of the Tel-Aviv area dialling code 03'.

'Like this book,' I said vaguely. Since Yitschak was silent I explained, 'A wise book is an advancing book. An advancing book is a book which develops advancing qualities. Forbearance, vigilance and precision are the qualifications which lead to enlightenment.'

'Are we going to be dealing next time with the *proper reading* of this wise book?'

'I have no objection to replacing this wise book with a different wise book.'

'Such as?'

'Bank balances, washing machine instructions or

a useful mathematical book such as the book of logarithms,' I replied, unimpressed by the expression of disgust on Yitschak's face. 'In the meantime,' I added, 'continue to exercise *proper reading* in this book of wisdom until our next meeting.'

'My teacher in school taught a different kind of proper reading,' said Yitschak.

'Your teacher taught proper reading for the first grade which is no longer your grade.'

'What is "proper reading" not for the first grade?' he asked.

'I've just demonstrated it to you.'

Yitschak was silent for a while and then spoke again, 'Not long ago, you hinted that the end of the trial period is approaching.'

'It is approaching,' I agreed, 'and to a great extent it depends on you – on your achievements.'

'On the *proper reading* of the telephone book?'

I nodded in agreement and added, 'Not necessarily of the telephone book; it could be any other wise book, but truly wise!'

'You mean terribly boring!'

'I mean, one which brings about advancing changes.'

It was late. I bid Yitschak farewell and returned home.

22

A touch of fear

According to my request, Yitschak came to pick me up from work.

'Today we must save time,' I said and explained. 'This evening we might be going out for a short walk which will end your trial period.'

'Is there a possibility that this walk will not take place?' Yitschak asked while stopping the car in front of a traffic light which had just turned red.

Since I did not answer immediately he saw fit to explain, 'You said *might*.' The amber traffic light caught his attention. The car moved slowly forward as we drove past the bustling, narrow road junction.

'Yes,' I replied, 'there is a possibility that our walk will be cancelled. It depends on our conversation this evening, and especially on the weather…'

'If it depends on the weather…' he said without turning his head since his eyes surveyed the narrow one-way street which was full of cars on both sides. His old car advanced sluggishly and carefully between them, giving a good-hearted rattle of protest which sounded like the purring of an old cat. As we drove out of this street, Yitschak was free to continue, 'If it really depends on the weather, its chances of taking place are zero.'

'Why?' I asked with surprise.

'Because there is a riotous wind, a drizzle here and there… the coastal strip is completely flooded and impossible to get through; the weather is defined as "stormy" and there is no hope of any change soon.'

Instead of replying, I wound down the window. The glass sank, creaking softly. It was obvious that everything possible had been done to silence those creaks, but to no avail. A strong wind burst into the driver's seat and dishevelled Yitschak's hair. It blew it from right to left, then backwards and eventually parted it in the middle. No doubt the wind must have treated my hair in the same mischievous manner, only it was short and therefore wouldn't yield as easily to the will of the wind. A piece of newspaper flew in the air and clung resolutely to Yitschak's ear.

'Mr S,' he cried, 'won't you please roll the window back up? I presume you've had enough time to determine what the weather is like… There is no chance that we will go out for a walk tonight,' he concluded.

'What brought you to this conclusion?'

'What you said. Didn't you say that our walk depends on the weather?'

'I did,' I agreed.

'Then our walk is cancelled,' Yitschak stated decidedly.

'On the contrary,' I said.

'Why?' Yitschak turned to me with a look of amazement in his eyes.

'I did not define *desirable* weather,' I replied.

'Do you mean that we would go out for a walk in this weather?'

'I mean that this particular weather is the suitable weather for our walk. If it doesn't change, we will take a walk along the beach tonight.'

Yitschak used our stop at the traffic lights to give me an inquisitive glance and it seemed to me that there was a touch of fear in his eyes.

23

Grasping
my very essence

It was quite early when we went up to Yitschak's room. The sun was sinking in the west and though lacking its crown of rays it still attempted to light the space that stretched between us. A blustering cloud of dust raged in that space and from time to time when the dust sank the white crests of huge billows were revealed to us.

Yitschak was not particularly encouraged by this sight. He stood still, peering anxiously through the porch window, as if his tense observation could change the intensity of the wind.

'Let's sit,' I said, reminding him that we hadn't yet carried out our half-hour of silence. He responded reluctantly and sat down at the other side of the table.

I easily disconnected.

Released of the last reminder of S, I filled the room with my infinite light. Who could grasp my very essence? I am in need of nothing. Those who yearn to reach me take endless trouble to penetrate my fundamental nature but as long as they have not awakened to knowing me they will not succeed. When they do, they will cease being what they imagined themselves to be.

All those corpses created by illusion are prevented from understanding that. Once they are released of the 'corpse-reality', that is, when they find themselves within me and become able to distinguish between the illusion and I – they will grasp my very essence. Then, they'll be freed of the 'frightened-corpse' image, chased by death – its lawful master – and become eternally free.

These words of mind are not written by me but by the one who is not I and yet is an inseparable part of me. My words here are intended for those brave human beings who went out in search of the true purpose of life, which is I.

S is trying to transfer my words faithfully but is prevented from doing so for he is not dealing with the transmission of things as they are but with a translation: a translation from a wordless language – the mother of all tongues. All languages from time immemorial are yearning to approach my language and inherit nothing but defeat.

S is trying to give those born blind an idea of the light and of the various colours. A day will come when this blind man will regain sight and be released of the enduring darkness in which he has remained since olden days. Then, when he is privileged to view the light in its full splendour, he will be full of laughter recalling the temporal concepts that attempted, in vain, to describe something of the truth.

Nevertheless, there is a point to those attempts, for they come to strengthen faith in the existence of the light, to lift up the spirit of those born blind and increase their vigilance towards the awakening, which is a matter of a split second. All of a sudden the light will flash and if the privileged one is not prepared for it and does not comprehend what is happening, he is liable to stay eternally in his blindness.

That's the reason why S has an important mission which he must fulfil thoroughly, with boundless devotion, through careful consideration and abnegation and with courage worthy of its name.

24

On the brink of
ending the trial period

Half an hour went by. As we have lately been accustomed, we did not hurry to start a conversation.

The crests of the huge mass of water, adorned with glittering strings of pure white foam, were touched lightly by the red ball of the sun.

Yitschak served hot tea in large cups with some dry cookies.

'I would like to pray,' he said.

Apparently, the fear had not abandoned him. He sensed that forthcoming events would exceed the bounds of the events in which he had taken part until now.

Before touching the tea we said a few verses from the Psalms. Yitschak's face was pale. He held his palms together with eyes half closed and prayed with humble devotion.

'Have you read Shankara's book?' I asked him.

'I have.'

'It is said there that as long as there is even a touch of fear in a man's heart, he is not Brahman.'

Yitschak made an attempt to smile and since he did not succeed he gave up and said seriously, 'I'm not Brahman.'

'You are walking the way leading to him; you must try to conquer the fear.'

'I used to try doing that even before I took the way you mentioned… but, as you know, one does not succeed in doing that by conversing over a cup of tea…'

'Fear is one of the basic attributes of the 'I'; it has no sense. You must not spare any effort in order to conquer it. Only a man who identifies with his body fears.'

'What does he fear?'

'Any damage that might be caused to the body, its inevitable extinction, pain, and the commonsense which repeatedly tells him that fear does not help the one who fears to become free of it.'

'Do you become free of fear once released of the "I"?'

'Utterly and eternally. The struggle against fear is the struggle against the "I". It's a struggle against hatred and jealousy which are no other than a result of fear. So fight your war!'

'And what about all those people who do not fight the "I" and the fear?'

'They pay the price – pain, grief, disappointment and the inevitable death.'

Yitschak pondered and since his reflections continued for a long time, I saw fit to point out, 'No one enforces upon another the choice of his way in life. Reaching where you are now was your own free choice.'

'And what if I choose to turn back the way I came?'

'No one can stop you.'

'Won't you try to stop me.'

'No.'

'Why?'

'Because I won't succeed. You are as strong as I am. The fundamental element that activates you is no

110

other than the element activating me or any other creature in this universe.'

'That element is...' Yitschak tried to guess and when he didn't succeed, I completed the sentence for him, 'The divinity, the divine spark, the eternity, Brahman – call it whatever you will. If my activator does not see fit to activate you, how can I resist him? It is he who decides for both of us. And indeed we are nothing but him, but that's already another story. At any rate,' I emphasized, 'you are free to decide how to act every minute of your life.'

'But you said that I lack the capacity of determination.'

'But not the capacity of decision,' I reminded him. 'You can make a decision and with the help of the forces assisting you, you may carry it out from planning to performance. However, those forces will desert you the minute you abandon the path to the absolute.'

'If so, then how would I be able to realize my decision to turn back?'

'Apparently, you do not need any assistance in order to turn back; you simply slide back to the abyss from which you have emerged with the force of inertia.'

'You are trying to influence me.'

'I am merely trying to describe the situation as it is. The final decision, as I said before, is entirely in your hands.'

Yitschak was pondering again when I announced, 'You have an hour and a half at your disposal. Let me know your decision.'

'Either we go out to end the trial period...' he whispered.

'Or we determine that it has already ended,' I emphasized.

'In failure,' Yitschak completed.

'In failure,' I agreed.

There was silence again in the room. I observed Yitschak. The black artery of carnal desire which curves in the lower part of the belly and climbs over the liver hasn't come to expression yet but undoubtedly expected its turn. I thought to myself: 'Even after our walk tonight more trials still await you, my boy.'

Yitschak cut off my thoughts, 'You said that the illusory world stems from the truth, that it is a sort of secretion, a kind of involuntary "sweat"…'

'That's right.'

'Sweat is secreted as a result of external conditions, like heat or humidity,' he said.

'The illusory world too is "secreted" from the reality in special external conditions,' I said.

'What are those "external conditions"?'

'The one and only reality.'

'You mean that the one and only reality influences itself and that's how the illusory world is created?'

'Precisely. There is no way of explaining it in the language of people who have not yet attained enlightenment.'

'Is there a language of people who have attained enlightenment?'

'Yes.'

'Which is it?'

'Silence.'

'Does this language possess the means for explaining the phenomenon?'

'There is no need to explain the obvious.'

'Are things obvious to the enlightened?'

'Yes.'

'How is that?'

'The enlightened *sees*,' I emphasized. 'You do not

need a description of the table in front of you but if you are born blind there are descriptions which might help you and there are things that are impossible to be described to you.'

'So again I have nothing to ask!'

'That would have been true if you were enlightened. But as long as you haven't attained enlightenment – ask. But mainly try to ask yourself, for all the answers are known to you.'

'All the answers are known to the enlightened,' he said.

'Every man is potentially enlightened, so all the answers are potentially known to him. He should make a little effort in order to activate his "potential" capabilities.'

'Make a *little* effort?' asked Yitschak.

'Very little. In fact, zero effort. Faith is enough.'

'Explain that!'

'All that a man on earth can do is equip himself with faith. Believe in the existence of the one reality with everything that stems from it. Believe that he is that reality and that only because he is sunk in a deep dream he has forgotten who he is and where he came from. Believe with absolute, unshakable faith every moment and everywhere. The rest will happen by itself.'

'That means that all those activities and trials are utterly unnecessary!'

'From the moment faith has been attained they are absolutey unnecessary. In fact, they are considered as "trials" only by the faithless person. For a man of faith they are merely amusing events.'

'What is the purpose of all those trials?'

'To arouse faith where it is absent and strengthen it where it exists.'

'How can you tell if there is such a chance.'

113

'By the willingness to stand trials.'

'But for the man of faith trials are not considered trials!'

'The man of faith is absolutely free of any fear.'

'He is the enlightened,' said Yitschak.

'The man of faith and the enlightened are one and the same. If you have achieved absolute faith – you have gained enlightenment. When achieving enlightenment, no matter how, you gain absolute faith. But pay attention, we are talking about *absolute faith*.'

'Who has attained absolute faith?'

'He whose heart has been swept clean of the last doubt. As I described to you the way to reaching the truth through "attachment to the relative truth", so does attachment to the relative faith lead to the absolute faith. That means forcing yourself to believe conditionally, until you are privileged to gain absolute faith.'

'Mr S, I'm trying to cling to faith and sweep away every shred of doubt from the darkened courtyard of my heart. Please get up and lead me to where you must!'

Since his statement was a little pathetic Yitschak tried to give it a tone of mockery but again he did not succeed; his voice was absolutely serious.

We drove to the deserted beach of Jaffa.

25

The faith and courage trial

It was late. The stars were invisible. A stormy wind whipped at us, spraying our faces with salty, shiveringly cold water. I stood still and silent, with Yitschak beside me. Suddenly the wind stopped completely. Time to act.

I turned to Yitschak. 'From here on you will go by yourself. Walk along the beach, carefully of course, but confidently and penetrate your heart with a firm belief that nothing will happen to you!' I emphasized and added, 'Walk for about two kilometres until you arrive at the third sewage pipe between Jaffa and Bat-Yam and wait for me there. Good luck!' I said and pushed him into the thick darkness. He wavered, stopped and hesitated for a moment. His body became rigid, then straightened up and was marched into the darkness which swallowed him at once.

I examined the stormy sea which roared like an aggravated beast of prey. Its billows had hardly left a passable stretch of beach. 'A test worthy of its name indeed,' I thought with satisfaction.

A vague memory rose in S's heart, a memory of a distant period when he used to march along the same beach every night in all weathers, more than once virtually risking his life. Now it all seemed ridiculous, like a children's game with lots of frightening masks, behind which well-intentioned aunts and uncles hide. At that time S was forced to muster up all his courage, faith and prayers in order to overcome the great fear which those stormy nights aroused in him, when surges suddenly rose before him like a wall, a few metres high, and a second later sank with a terrifying bubbling sound, opening a dark bottomless abyss at his feet. And those stray dogs, lurking behind a rock, merging into its shadow and all of a sudden leaping forth straight into his face. And the straying madmen wandering about, pestering him…

I was about to walk up the hill and reach the meeting place by the dry, short route. Before climbing, I wanted to determine Yitschak's precise location and see how he was. I saw him at the foot of the wall, near the second sewage pipe. He was surrounded by bubbling billows that leaped up to five metres above him. I pondered for a moment.

As far as that puppet of meat named 'Yitschak' was concerned, it was possible to define the situation as 'dangerous'. The danger was in the fact that the fleshly existence of that creature was liable to be stopped. In other words, maybe these were Yitschak's last hours or possibly his last minutes…

I looked around in an attempt to locate a solemn image dressed in black which is tightly connected to this world and in cases such as this one stands beside the person in danger in order to bring his conventional existence to a perfect completion – in other words, which are indeed conventional and yet somewhat poetic – 'to take his breath away'. I didn't notice it and the truth must be told – I was surprised. There were such waves and Yitschak was standing on a piece of slippery rock and despite that, these were not his last moments! You might say that a special feeling rose in S: a feeling which some time ago he would have defined as a 'feeling of relief'.

The darkness around defied description. A wide smile spread across my face. In my mind, I could picture Yitschak sitting in front of me and describing the various emotions he had experienced in this extraordinary situation. And just then, I noticed the familiar tall solemn image. It stood halfway in the distance between Yitschak and myself, approximately thirty metres high.

'Is that so?' I asked myself and then directed my question to it. 'That's right,' was the silent answer. 'It isn't exactly the destined hour but it could very well be... As you know, there is considerable room for manoeuvre – if no last-minute change occurs...'

I decided to rush to Yitschak's aid, even at the cost of some undesirable consequence for me and possibly for him too. I directed a thought-wave at the piece of rock where Yitschak stood and was instantly standing beside him.

He refused to believe his eyes. All wet, he stared at me with his mouth wide open. A breaker shattered his balance and threw him at my feet. I stretched out my hand to him and he clutched at it with spasmodically trembling hands. I directed myself at the wave that was approaching us and asked it to lift us up to the wall.

The wave rose, made a friendly rumbling sound, detached itself from the black mass, lowered itself and then, with a courageous swing, lifted us up onto its shining hump. We experienced the pleasant sensation aroused when the giant wheel at the amusement park swings you way up high.

A second passed.

We were both standing on the wall. A bubbling chasm yawned beneath us. We were out of danger. I

117

sent my gratitude to the sea and turned to Yitschak. He ran towards the hill in search of shelter. I walked behind him.

Yitschak squeezed himself into a narrow crevice, sheltered from the wind and rain – which suddenly started lashing – and made room for me too. His body was trembling and his clothes were torn. Water was streaming from his hair, dripping from the tip of his nose, ears and chin. The shivering of his body grew stronger and his knees seemed to be knocking.

'You tried to trick me,' he cried, attempting to put on a mischievous smile, but instead started shivering uncontrollably. His teeth chattered madly despite his attempt to overcome this.

'You followed me, and I didn't notice you,' he stuttered with no attempt to smile. The expression on his face was that of fright and his teeth were still chattering.

'And at the right moment you stood beside me… How did you do that?' he said with exaggerated surprise and seemed to overcome his shivering. 'You must have been walking quite close to me and I didn't even feel it! In fact, I looked back quite a few times but didn't see a thing, except a wall of thick darkness… You've fooled me,' he said, trying again to give his voice an amused tone. 'Tell me,' he asked suddenly and his teeth started chattering again, 'are you a sorcerer?' Then with an attempt to prevent any chance of an answer from me or maybe from himself he quickly continued, 'How lucky we were with that wave! If it weren't for it, there would be nothing left of us both! In the ephemeral sense, of course!' he remembered to add, trying to smile once again. As a result, his face had the expression of a bird, more precisely an owl. It aroused my laughter. 'Ha ha ha, ho ho ho!' my voice echoed loudly. 'Ha ha ha, boom

boom boom!' the stormy sea answered me from the distance, as the mighty masses of water shook the steep stretch of beach. I laughed again, and again the sea replied. Yitschak just stood there baffled.

26
The world as an 'agreed-upon' picture

We made our way through a thorny field, down to the road and walked towards the car. When we were comfortably seated inside, Yitschak sighed deeply. A second later he tried to imitate my laughter. The result was a colourless sound like an old man's cough.

'Aha,' he finally uttered with a twisted smile, 'we have seen the angel of death.'

'True,' I responded seriously, 'we have!'

Yitschak raised his head. Underneath his wet eyebrows, his eyes examined my features with tension and anxiety. He turned to me and spoke, weighing his words carefully, 'Mr S, I wasn't serious!'

I couldn't help the laughter that the tension on his face aroused in me. He was embarrassed.

'What weren't you serious about?' I asked.

'The angel of death,' he replied.

'But it is the most serious image on the face of this earth!'

'I mean,' Yitschak remarked with a kind of terror in his eyes, 'when I said that "we have seen the angel of death" – I didn't mean it seriously…'

'But he was there!' I said.

'But we haven't seen him!' cried Yitschak, trying to convince me, or maybe himself, by raising his voice.

'We saw him. You admitted it yourself!'

'I was joking.'

'Don't joke about the angel of death,' I warned him, lifting my finger as bursts of laughter accompanied my speech.

'Did you see him?' Yitschak demanded firmly.

'Of course, and so did you.'

'I did not. I mentioned him just by chance.'

I restrained my laughter, swallowed, and said, 'Listen here, my boy,' then I went silent for a moment in order to recover my breath. 'Chance is a word without meaning. There is no place for *chance* in the illusory world; if there were, it would have already collapsed. What holds it together and makes it 'real', so to speak, is its magnificent order. Everything is calculated, everything runs the course it was meant to and arrives at its predetermined destination. If a man thinks of something – it isn't by chance. In terms of the world he is living in, it is the sure and sound truth. If a man thinks of palaces and magnificent vehicles, it means that they are either around him or that he is about to reach them. If a man is constantly bothered by thoughts of some disease, it means that it's either around him or that he is about to have it; furthermore, if a man is compelled to think about a particular subject, such as palaces or a malignant disease, he will end up receiving it. You don't joke about such things.'

Yitschak shook himself out of his astonishment, 'And if, for instance, a man focused his thought on recovering from that malignant disease?'

'Then he would recover.'

'Impossible.'

'If a man repeatedly says to himself – "I am well" for a whole week, twenty-four hours a day – he will recover.'

121

'Even when he is asleep?'

'Even when he is asleep, he should make an effort to say it in his dreams.'

'Tell that to someone who's sick with cancer.'

'He will not recover.'

'Why?'

I twisted myself so that my back touched the car's closed window and my face was turned towards Yitschak. Weighing the words, I said, 'Because he is unable to detach himself from the picture.'

'What picture?'

'The one drawn in his mind through generations. If you like, you can regard the world of illusion as a series of pictures that were agreed upon in advance. These agreed-upon pictures reveal that no man is cured of a malignant disease. This is a concept which is planted in a man's mind along with its very creation, like a kind of heredity, a matter of genes. A man of such consciousness might say "I'm well" but deep down in his heart he will still be absolutely certain that this is not true and could not be true since he has a malignant disease. All that, because of the agreed-upon picture in his mind. He will get well if he succeeds in exceeding the bounds of that agreed-upon picture.'

'What is the meaning of "exceeding the bounds of that agreed-upon picture"?'

'To awaken to knowing himself as that which he really is. To attain enlightenment.'

'Does someone who has attained enlightenment get cured of a malignant disease?'

'No.'

Yitschak was confused. He scratched the palm of his hand which was still wet, and remarked, 'You have just said the opposite: "If the enlightened says I'm well – he will get well."'

'If he says – he will. But he won't say.'

'Why?'

'Because his interest in the body has come to an absolute end. It died. If you had imagined that a certain car was marvellous and reliable, and all of a sudden found out that it is a paper car, would you continue to be interested in it as before? Would you still go on taking care of its spare parts, oil and fuel?'

'But the enlightened does eat, walk, rest and obey nature's law.'

'Mechanically, out of habit. One does not smash or tear apart the paper car; one lets it disintegrate in due course. After all, it can be hung on a wall, put into a gold frame so that its appearance may be admired!'

'But should he nevertheless say – "I'm well"?' insisted Yitschak.

'Then he will,' I calmed him down and added, 'That is, his body will, but as I said before, he won't say that.'

'Is it worth aspiring to enlightenment at all?'

I shrugged my shoulders. Yitschak started his car.

27

'Here' and 'There'

Yitschak came to pick me up. Heavy rain was lashing the old Peugeot's windows.

'Winter is at its peak,' remarked Yitschak.

I did not say a word. It was cosy in the car.

'It's pleasant in here,' Yitschak said as if reading my mind.

'The truth is,' I replied, 'that there is no difference between "here" and "there".'

'By *there* you mean outside?'

'Yes.'

'I wouldn't like to stand outside in the pouring rain. As far as I'm concerned, it's much better to sit in here.'

'That's because you identify yourself with your body and its passing sensations. When you are no longer dependent upon those sensations, when *here* and *there* – the rain outside and the warmth in the car – are the same for you, then you'll be very close to enlightenment.'

'It seems to me that only when I am actually enlightened, I'll feel this way.'

'When you are enlightened you'll be able to feel however you wish to feel... At your wish the cold and the heat will be one and the same; at your wish the heat will be pleasant and the cold unpleasant or vice versa, whatever you please. But when you are very close to enlightenment – just like a man who digs into the ground in order to find a treasure, and all of a sudden the handle of the longed-for crate is revealed before his very eyes – then cold and heat will be just the same for you because you'll be whole-heartedly given to the glorious feeling of growing closer to the absolute light.'

We were driving along that narrow one-way street which was packed with cars on both sides. The engine often stalled, grunting in desperate protest. The rain stopped for a few minutes and then started again, whipping against the car windows even more fiercely. The windscreen wipers were working but didn't always manage to overcome the torrent.

28
The yearning
for absolute freedom

Yitschak had heated his room beforehand with a two-bar electric fire. After the half-hour silence we drank some hot, fragrant tea in large cups with some plum jam to sweeten it.

'How did you all of a sudden stand next to me the other night?' Yitschak asked.

'Have you ever seen children sailing paper boats in the river?'

'In the movies.'

'The boat bumps into obstacles and sometimes turns over and is lost. But sometime the chain of events is different.'

'And so?'

'It is pulled to a safe shore with the help of a stick.'

'Meaning I am the boat and you are the stick?'

'You and I are the boat-builders who identify themselves with the boats completely. Nevertheless, we are not the boats themselves. At certain moments we can disconnect ourselves from the hypnotic identification and do with the boats whatever we please.'

'Pull them up to a safe shore?'

'If that is indeed what had occurred to us.'

'But that is not according to the rules of the game…'

'We invent the game and we determine its rules.'

'Could anyone "detach himself from the hypnotic identification" and pull his boat onto a safe shore?'

'Anyone who gained knowledge of the art of detachment.'

'Could the one who gained that knowledge pull up the boat of the one who hadn't yet gained it?'

'He could, but it isn't recommended.'

'Why?'

'Because he changes the rules, which he is entitled to do, but the results of his action cause embarrassment and confusion within entire systems.'

Yitschak considered my answer and although he did not seem satisfied, he asked no more. After a short silence he said, 'I've changed after that night. I used to go and play billiards on Saturday nights but now I have no interest in the game and prefer to sit at home alone. I used to put girls on a pedestal once. Now, I try to catch their eye. In the morning I get up all fresh and awake and most of the time there is some secret joy in my heart… What is the meaning of all this?'

'The experiment stage is over. Now you are like a man who has made his choice, bought his weapon, examined it and practised with it, and now is ready for battle.'

'Are there also losers in this battle?'

'Nine hundred and ninety-nine out of a thousand lose and need additional lifetime in order to prepare and get ready again. Obviously, then their way is shorter and easier but that doesn't mean you essentially belong to the nine hundred and ninety-nine… Maybe you are the lucky one. After all, he too exists!'

I chuckled mischievously.

'You won't succeed in discouraging me, Mr S! I'm encouraged by the change in myself. Even if I fail my steps in the future, this change is enough for me. Is this achievement vulnerable too?'

'Not always. Some lose everything and some retain their achievements until their next lifetime, but that is on one condition…'

'Which is?'

'That death snatches them in the midst of battle before they have been totally defeated.'

'In other words, the loss is total!' said Yitschak with a touch of grief in his voice.

'Nevertheless, something still remains.'

'What?'

'The foundations. Nothing can destroy them. Laying the foundations is not easy but from the moment they have been laid, they are yours forever. You can always reconstruct once you have solid foundations under your feet.'

'Have I those foundations?' Yitschak asked anxiously.

'Man,' I replied, raising my voice, 'you've been standing on them for quite some time now.'

'Then I have a point of departure.'

'Which is for ever unshakable. You cannot return to being without foundation, that is, lacking the yearning for absolute freedom.'

'Is the yearning for absolute freedom the foundation?'

'It is the very solid foundation of absolute freedom without which you will never gain freedom. With it, whatever defeats you may suffer, you'll end up achieving that which you have yearned for. Defeats are only a delay in time.'

'In other words, I belong to those people who will not rest until they are free from the enslavement to the illusory world!'

'Welcome into their congregation!' I made a wide

theatrical hand movement and bowed, bending down like a loyal servant, inviting his master's guests to a magnificent feast thrown in their honour.

'And what if I wished to rid myself of these foundations?' Yitschak asked on the spur of the moment.

'You'd never want that.'

'But still, what if I did?' insisted Yitschak.

'They are the very essence of your existence; you cannot break off from freedom in order to get into freedom; you can never give it up.'

'You mean the yearning for freedom.'

'Yes.'

'Why?'

'From the moment something real and true comes into the world – however much you turn it over and over – it will stand forever!'

'Is that how the absolute came into the world?'

'The absolute did not come into the world; the world is emitted from it. Only he who has become enlightened and awakened to knowing the absolute does not ask questions.'

'Does he understand everything?'

'"Understanding" does not exist in the perception system of the enlightened; there is something that is beyond understanding, which is not "understanding" in the common sense of the word.'

'My questions are probably not very clever,' Yitschak apologized. 'Nevertheless, I shall dare to ask two more questions: What is the purpose of the illusion that's "exuded" by the absolute? And what is your role concerning me?'

'Ha ha ha ha…' I burst into a deafening laughter. 'Ha ha ha ha… Ho ho ho ho! You are asking what time is it? It's eight thirty-one according to my watch and it's time you drove me home!'

29
You are
your own guide

Again, we were sitting in front of the steaming cups of tea while a nice winter day had slowly come to an end. Yitschak's electric heater was burning its two coils.

'Why are you in the habit of evading answers sometimes?' he asked me.

I sipped the tea slowly and calmly, examined the yellow wall beside me thoroughly, and, smiling widely, I replied, 'I assure you that I have never evaded an answer to any question whatsoever!'

'Last week, instead of giving me an answer you laughed in my face.'

'Not instead of an answer,' I corrected him.

'You mean, the laughter was the answer?'

'If it followed the question, then that was the only answer I could find at that moment.'

'But it did not mean a thing to me!'

I shrugged my shoulders. 'That's nobody's fault.'

'Could you guide me towards understanding these special answers – give me a key?'

'A key to laughing?'

'Yes.'

'Laugh!'

'What do you mean *laugh*?'

'You asked for a "key".'

130

'Is that the key?'

'Yes.'

'That I should laugh?'

'Yes.'

'And then everything will become clear to me?'

'Completely and utterly.'

He looked at me with total disbelief and, all of a sudden, blew his cheeks up and produced some vague and quite strange sounds which he soon stopped.

'Strange,' he said, 'I can't laugh!'

'You can't understand!'

'Will I ever understand?'

'When the time comes – you will.'

'Will I laugh?'

'Ha ha ha ha! Ho ho ho ho!' I burst into a roar of loud and clear laughter.

Yitschak looked at me astounded. He tried to imitate me again and suffered a crushing defeat. I went on laughing until there were tears in my eyes. I wiped them off with the back of my hand and looked at Yitschak with amusement, 'Try tickling yourself,' I suggested seriously. He thought for a minute, examining me, and since he did not notice any muscle movement on my face that would reveal even the slightest hint of mischievousness, he tickled his arm-pits like a baby.

The serious expression on my face was at once shattered and I was swept away by a strong, long, sweeping laughter. Yitschak looked at me with wide-open eyes. His hands were still in the air, close to his armpits.

'Laugh,' I urged him. 'Laugh!'

'You were making fun of me!'

'Laugh like me,' I urged him.

'I can't,' he sighed and added desperately, 'but I do laugh sometimes.'

131

'Then you do not ask questions.'

'You mean because all the answers are known to me then?'

'No, because the laughter shuts your mouth!' I replied and went on laughing: 'Ha ha ha ha! Ho ho ho ho!...'

When I stopped laughing, Yitschak tried teasing me, 'You find it difficult to control your outburst of laughter!'

'I can't control them! Free men are unable to control their freedom. If they could, they would have become enslaved again.'

'I'm confused!' admitted Yitschak.

'Let's sit in silence for another half an hour,' I suggested.

We plunged into silence. I could feel how the waves of grievance and rage in Yitschak's heart calmed down. Peace was restored. Then I disconnected.

When I returned to S I saw Yitschak standing in front of me, trying to attract my attention by waving his palms before my eyes in a movement that is usually used to check the eyesight of a baby. When he noticed the slight movement on my face, he stopped, sighed and said, 'Mr S, it's ten-thirty; you've been sitting for more than five hours!'

'Well, it's late then.'

'Not for me. I can drive you, but first... if you please, just one more question... and I would like to get a verbal answer... I still can't grasp the meaning of the other kind of answers – as clever as they might be.'

'Ask.'

'What is your role concerning me? Why did you agree to guide me?'

'I have never agreed to guide you. I have no

idea if I can guide myself, let alone others. You are imagining that my role is to be your guide.'

'Isn't it true?' Yitschak interrupted my speech with a hint of anxiety in his eyes.

'You are your own guide and that's why I'm standing by your side. As to the other question: "What is the purpose of the illusion emitted by the absolute to the absolute" – which I indeed answered but you did not seem to grasp my answer – here is an answer of your favourite kind: the illusion is the touchstone of the absolute which proves its being absolute. Only the absolute who experienced the illusion and disconnected from it knows that he is indeed absolute. Are you ready to drive me?'

30
The way
to know truth

A week later, we were sitting again at Yitschak's place for the half-hour of silence.

While drinking tea Yitschak informed me that he had started to write down my answers. 'This will give me time to delve into them,' he said. Since I did not respond he added, 'Why does the absolute need a touchstone?"

'It does not need it,' I replied.

He gave me a critical look out of the corner of his eye and continued, 'Last week you claimed that "the illusion is the *touchstone* of the absolute which proves its being absolute".'

'I do not notice the word *need* anywhere here,' I said.

'Later you said, "only the absolute who experienced the illusion and disconnected from it knows that he is indeed absolute". That means,' Yitschak clarified, 'that in order for the absolute to know that he is absolute, he needs to experience the illusion and disconnect from it.'

'And what about the absolute who doesn't want to know anything?'

'So there are two kinds of "absolute"?'

'There are zero kinds of "absolute".'

'Does that mean that the absolute does not exist?'

'No, it does not exist.'

'What does exist then?'

'You and I.'

'But we are no more than passing flesh!'

'As an absolute, we are immortal!'

'You are making fun of me! You said that the absolute does not exist!'

I burst into laughter, 'My honourable Mr Yitschak,' I said, 'I may say whatever I wish. I may talk in my sleep. What has that got to do with the absolute?'

'I want to know the truth!'

'There is a well-proven way to do that.'

'Which is?'

'Keep your mouth shut. The more it's shut – the closer you are to the truth. The more you prattle – the farther you are from it.'

'You prattle too!'

'Listen, my boy, listen carefully!… or should I say, hurry up and write down what I tell you now? You are incapable of hearing what I'm saying!'

'How come?' Yitschak wondered while rushing to take a pen and paper. 'I don't understand!'

'You are incapable of hearing what I'm telling you!'

'Why?'

'Because you are deaf! And worst of all, you don't realise that you are!'

'Mr S, I give up!' Yitschak withdrew his intention of writing down my speech. 'It seems to me that I can hear you and now you claim that I'm deaf!'

'I repeat and say: you, Yitschak, are as deaf as a doorpost! And you'll do very well to engrave that on your heart. You do not hear me. Everything you seem to hear is nothing but a figment of your own imagination! If someday your ears open and you hear – you will fall off your feet with laughter at yourself!' As I burst into roars of laughter I added, 'The boy sits there, asking a question and imagining that he hears an answer, and on that basis he builds himself a whole world made of "hot air"!'

Yitschak was alarmed. Profound disappointment arose in his eyes as he asked, 'Do you mean to say that there wasn't any truth in everything you told me until today?'

'There was nothing but truth in everything I told you until today,' I stated and immediately added, 'The question is – to what extent can someone who is deaf and dumb to the truth grasp words of truth?'

'Who is capable of grasping words of truth?'

'The truth. When you cease to be "Yitschak" and become Truth, your ears will be opened to perceive what I'm saying.'

'And until then?'

'Recognise your deafness. Stop prattling with your questions. Be humble and anticipate salvation! Your hour will come! Be prepared and hope for it with all your heart; it will not linger – it will come! I give you my word of honour!'

31

The surprise

Time went by as rainy winter days followed one another. Since Yitschak's mental capacity changed and increased as a result of that stormy night on the beach, I was expecting to see the kind of new challenge he would bring upon himself. I anticipated something extraordinarily powerful and indeed it was not long before it arrived.

It was a clear bright afternoon. Yitschak came to meet me at the gate of my workplace with a radiant face.

'I have a surprise for you,' he said. 'It's waiting for you at home!'

I got into the car and rested my elbow on the open window. A soft, refreshing breeze was blowing rhythmically. I gazed at Yitschak. There was no trace left of that black 'vessel' of carnal desire. Instead, he was surrounded by a kind of dark red, almost brown glow.

'Can you guess what the surprise is?' he asked, changing gear quickly and speeding up.

'A woman,' I determined, half amused and half indifferent.

A sharp scream of brakes was Yitschak's instant response. The car stopped in the middle of the road. Angry drivers went past us, going out of their way in order to throw at us a variety of colourful curses, accompanied with meaningful gestures.

'How did you know?' Yitschak asked, unable to control the outward manifestations of his astonishment – pale face, wide-open mouth and eyes coming out of their sockets.

'The stars informed me.'

'Was it just a guess?' he asked, attempting to calm down.

'What else could it have been? Start your car, we are blocking the traffic!' I said.

We drove in silence for a while and then Yitschak opened his heart. 'She is a girl I used to know a long time ago. We were neighbours, you see; our parents lived in the Rechavia neighbourhood in Jerusalem. Her father is a professor in the faculty of political science in the Hebrew University.'

'What does your father do?'

'He is a professor of psychology. My grandfather was a geologist like his father.'

'The one who bequeathed the Chinese plate to you?'

'That's the one.'

'So you broke the tradition of academic education...'

'I'm allowed to. My eldest brother is studying psychology and I have a sister who is a biologist. We were at elementary school with Eve... and also two years at secondary school. We were considered lovers and indeed there was something between us, only we were both shy. Later I moved here, to Tel-Aviv... I was in conflict with my parents. I graduated from vocational school here. Then I was drafted and completed my regular military service. A year later the Yom Kippur War[9] broke out and I was sent first to the south and then to the north. This war raised

138

many questions in my heart which hung in empty darkness. Then I came across your translations and it seemed to me that the right answers to my questions were beginning to burst forth... I forgot all about her... Her name is Eve.'

'Eve?' I asked, bored.

'Oh, you are probably wondering why a professor from Jerusalem would give his daughter such a name.[10] Well, her mother is English.' The engine made its regular hum as Yitschak went past a traffic light. He drove fast for a while, made a sharp turn and then eased his pressure on the accelerator.

'We met a month ago. It was a kind of revelation: everything was swept away from my heart and she was all that was left in it. It was as if I was revived into a new life. It obviously disturbed me a little in the contemplation. You see, her image kept appearing all the time... and instead of the words I had to think about I heard her voice. Do you think it will hold me back?'

'A little. Be diligent with the contemplation, even if there is nothing left of it.'

'What is the meaning of *there is nothing left of it*?'

'If you don't manage to concentrate even for a second on your contemplation – subject.'

'What's the point in such contemplation?'

'As long as you continue to do it, whatever happens to you or disturbs you is only an obstacle which sooner or later will be cleared out of your way. If you cease to carry it out your defeat is complete. Don't stop contemplating!'

[9] The war of 1973 which started on the Jewish day of atonement, called 'Yom Kippur'.
[10] In Hebrew Eve is Chava or Hava.

139

'I can promise you that!'

'Don't promise me; promise yourself!'

We approached the narrow, familiar street which, to my surprise, was not packed with cars today, probably because people had gone out to enjoy the nice winter day.

'Last week Eve and I decided to tell you and surprise you... She is waiting for us in my room... Your guess spoiled everything!' he said and uttered a nervous giggle.

'What is it that you've decided to tell me about?'

'The revival of our connection. There is a lot of purity and innocence in it.'

'Only in absolute freedom is there purity and innocence,' I remarked.

'Please! You don't understand.'

'Did you say *connection*?'

'Yes.'

'*Connection* is a word contradictory to *purity* and *innocence*. Wherever a connection exists, purity and innocence do not. Anyone who ties another with any bond whatsoever is neither innocent nor pure.'

Yitschak parked the car and we walked into the drafty, dim entrance of the building. He did not perceive my last words. Once more his face lit up with momentary joy and again I noticed that red-brownish aura which surrounded him. It was about half a metre wide. We climbed up the old staircase. As usual, he ran ahead to open the door of his rented room before me. I entered. The room was empty.

'Eve!' Yitschak called. 'Eve! You can come out. He guessed everything!'

A shadow detached itself from the dim corner of the small kitchen and seconds later a young woman stood before me. As far as harmony of shape,

140

brightness of complexion and the expression of the eyes went, it could be said that her creator had done a good job. It was easy to imagine Yitschak's powerful attachment to her. He was exposed to a quick, deadly cross-fire, completely unprotected.

S, who was aware of me, could see the 'biographical' evolution of the young woman: a woman in full bloom, a mature woman whose first tiny wrinkles at the edges of the eyes had become apparent; an elderly woman with a face all shrivelled with wrinkles, which made it hard to recognise its beauty in bygone days; a very old woman whose skin hung loose over her bones and… ashes, probably because in her day bodies would be burnt instead of buried or possibly because she would perish in a fire.

'Yitschak told me about you,' she said extending a delicate hand. I shook the hand and looked into her eyes. They expressed subtle desire, a well-developed sense of beauty, perception and composure on one hand, and a willingness to submit to passionate sensations on the other. Some more contrasts were disguised by a good-hearted mischievousness, a lot of curiosity, and an apparent attempt to determine my nature.

Her glance, bravely directed at me at first, soon subsided and retreated. It was transformed into astonishment and then awe. Its brightness disappeared and before I could perceive what was behind it, it turned aside. I pulled my hand from hers which was squeezing mine as though asking for support.

'I've already told him about you, since he guessed what the surprise was.' Yitschak hurried to justify himself.

'Did you really guess, Mr S?' the girl asked, this time displaying sincere surprise followed by a flow of admiration that was captivating with its childish charm. I amused myself playing with it. The charm went through the curves of my brain tissue and disappeared without leaving a trace. A second wave penetrated my chest, went through the heart area and since it did not achieve any reaction whatsoever, it too vanished. The source of charm concluded that there was no point in additional projection and, absorbing what had been classified as a defeat in its consciousness, stopped the flow. The look in Eve's eyes was cold and black.

'Yitschak surely told you,' I said amiably, 'that our meetings begin with half an hour of silence.'

'How very interesting!' Eve expressed her admiration.

'But today, Mr S...' Yitschak started to stutter.

'Is a day like any other day,' I interrupted him with a smile and took my usual place at one end of the table. Yitschak gave Eve a look of helplessness and she came to his aid. 'I'd like to try that! I have some idea of meditation, only at the moment I have no subject... Would you give me one?' she asked me.

'Count your breath.'

'Count my breath? How?'

'One, two, three, four,' I demonstrated, inhaling the air at each count.

'How much should I count?'

'Until half an hour has passed.'

'It will be an astronomical figure!'

'Not so astronomical,' I laughed. 'A person breathes about eighteen times per minute. Multiply that by thirty and you'll get five hundred and forty. Presuming your breathing is faster than usual, you'll arrive at six hundred.'

'Why didn't I think of that?' Eve clapped her hands, surprised and ashamed. 'Let's go, Mr S!'

I immediately disconnected.

I re-activated S early, after approximately twenty-five minutes. Yitschak and the girl were having a silent conversation. Yitschak noticed the change in my face which foretold the end of my contemplation and saw fit to make a justification. 'She couldn't last out! It's her first time… After all, she is a guest!' He smiled evasively but failed to conceal his embarrassment.

I thought to myself, 'Could he have brought upon himself a challenge which is beyond his ability to handle…?'

'I heard that you are accustomed to going out for walks along the beach,' Eve said in her high-pitched, pleasant voice. I noticed Yitschak's reaction: his whole 'being' – thought-waves and a variety of emotions flew towards the girl and surrounded her with a kind of large red cloud.

'Yes,' I said, 'we are used to going out for walks in the fresh air.'

'Shall we go out for a little walk today too?' she asked mischievously, trying again to examine me closely, but as soon as her glance crossed mine she withdrew immediately and spoke looking down.

'I'm sure Mr S will agree,' Yitschak urged me and added, 'it's the first really nice winter day. What light! The air is transparent and the beach is clean!' He was standing by the porch window. I did not reply. Yitschak turned to me and gave me a look that pleaded: 'Please don't spoil it!'

'We are accustomed to going out for work-walks,' I said with a smile.

'Yitschak didn't tell me… what are work-walks?'

'There's still some hope,' I thought to myself, amused.

'As far as you are concerned it is just a walk,' Yitschak hurried to explain.

'There is no such thing as "just a walk",' I cut in decisively. Yitschak was alarmed and gave up the next part of the sentence, 'For us, it is a work-walk.'

'I'm a little confused,' the girl admitted, 'but if you'll permit me, I'll join you in your work-walk which for me, as Yitschak said, is just a walk.'

'And a pleasant one,' I complemented Yitschak with an attempt to encourage her.

We went down to the beach.

For this time of the year it was unusual to find people on the beach. There were fishermen and some couples of various ages, who strolled embracing each other. There were also a few people who went out to enjoy the setting of the beautiful day by themselves.

After twenty minutes of calm walking which was decorated with the delicious, almost poetic, conversation of Eve and Yitschak, and with my short remarks, I stood still and turned to Yitschak. 'Do you still remember how to pray in public?' His face suddenly paled and his smile froze. Eve sensed his embarrassment and tried to encourage him. 'Praying in public must be very interesting. My grandfather used to do it,' she said cheerfully and turned to Yitschak. 'Surely you remember it well!' Turning to me she asked, 'How do you do it?'

'By kneeling down and saying verses of the Psalms.'

'I have never seen or heard of anyone kneeling down[11] in a synagogue while saying verses of the Psalms but maybe it's more noble and sincere this way... only I don't see any synagogue in the vicinity!' She turned her gaze towards the street, searching

---

[11] Jews conduct their prayer in a synagogue standing up, not kneeling down.

for a house that might resemble a synagogue among the peeling buildings.

'We don't need a synagogue,' I said.

'You mean we should go back home?' Eve asked and added in a coquettish tone, 'But we've only just come out!'

'That wasn't my intention.'

'Where would you kneel down then?' The girl expressed obvious surprise.

'Right here,' I said with a fatherly smile and pointed at the light coloured piece of beach where we stood.

She turned to Yitschak with complete disbelief. He lowered his head and nodded in confirmation.

'Do you really intend to do that?'

'Yes,' I answered and added, 'and not for the first time.'

'As far as I'm concerned,' Yitschak saw fit to explain, 'it is only the second time.' The excitement in his voice was that of someone whose thoughts were in turmoil.

She studied him closely, her look expressing pity and alarm at the same time, then she said decisively, 'I'll wait for you tomorrow by the front gate of the university, at the same time…'

'Two-thirty,' Yitschak uttered gloomily.

'Two-thirty,' she confirmed.

She waved to him with her delicate hand. 'See you!' she called and left the beach in tiny but quick steps. I knelt down, joined my hands and looked up to the sky, 'I thank you, my Lord…' I started murmuring. From the corner of my eye I saw the girl's silhouette: she stood still for a moment, gazed at me and then started running. A second later I felt Yitschak kneeling beside me.

Most of the people who witnessed the scene

hastened their steps to get away from us but there were a few hooligans who were attracted and slowly formed a wide circle around us. When I stood up, followed by Yitschak, I counted about five youngsters aged between fifteen and twenty-five.

'You're Moslems, eh?' shouted one of them.

'Christians,' uttered the one next to him confidently and, shoving his elbows into his friend's ribs, added in a noisy voice which was meant to tease, 'The Christians are the ones who kneel down and pray with their hands together!'

The youngest of them tried to imitate me. He knelt down on the sand and started twisting and distorting his body while sending an unctuous look towards the sky. I approached him, attached his palms to one another, lifted his head up by the chin and commanded, 'Now pray!'

He was embarrassed, 'What? How?' he asked. 'How do you pray?'

'Ask God for something and you'll receive it!' I said. He looked at me doubtfully.

'If I ask to be rich and handsome?' he asked with a giggle which covered up much tension.

'Then you'll be rich and handsome,' I said confidently, 'if you promise him that you will not abuse your wealth and beauty.'

The youngster closed his eyes and started murmuring with devotion. The rest of the youngsters became serious. Another one attempted to kneel down but changed his mind at the last minute and stood back up, brushing the sand from his trousers and shouting mockingly, 'Rubbish!' His remark did not gain any support.

'Who knows?' remarked the oldest of them pensively. He was a short, dark-haired youth with broad shoulders. A third lad came up to me and said, 'I can't

146

kneel down… but I believe. Would you bless me?'

'What would you like to be blessed with?'

'That my mother will get well and my father will get rich.'

'Ask for wealth for yourself; it's much safer!' commented the youngster who had tried to kneel down and changed his mind.

'If my father is rich, then I will be rich too,' answered the lad, but added, 'Well, OK bless me too with wealth!' He bent his head down a little and held his palms together while closing his eyes. I put my palm over his head and blessed him.

The gang dispersed.

I sat down on the sand that was still warm from the setting sun. Yitschak approached me and sat heavily next to me. We were silent for a long while. After the sun had set completely and the soft breeze started increasing the frequency of its gusts, he broke the silence and said, 'She studies medicine. She preferred to study in Tel-Aviv instead of Jerusalem…'

'Because of you,' I said. 'You are in love with each other.'

'We love one another…'

'No,' I emphasized, 'you don't *love* one another but are *in love*, by way of all flesh.'

'Is there any difference?' Yitschak wondered, surprised.

'Unfathomable. But we'll talk about that some other time.'

'When?'

'Not in the near future, if ever.'

He said nothing.

After a long silence Yitschak asked in a clear voice that concluded a piercing inner dialogue, 'What actually is the purpose of the woman?'

'She is the last fortress of the "I".'

147

'Do you mean to say that women do not gain enlightenment?'

'Women do gain enlightenment.'

'If they are the very "I"…'

'That I did not say,' I interrupted him.

'If they are the last fortress of the "I"…?'

'That doesn't mean that they are the "I" itself.'

'How could women gain enlightenment?'

'The same way men do.'

'Triumph over the "I"?'

'Yes.'

'But they are its fortress?'

'It is essential to break down the fortress.'

'That means – to overthrow themselves.'

'To overthrow the woman in them,' I clarified.

'What is a *woman*?' Yitschak was wise enough to ask.

'Power which is nurtured by the weakness of others.' And before I'd be asked another question I explained, 'Sexual attraction. A man who can over-come sexual attraction is capable of overcoming the enslaving power of the *woman*.'

'Isn't she interested in such men?'

'Such men give her back her self-respect and freedom.'

'As what?'

'As someone who does not need the power that sexual attraction imparts. From the moment a woman gives up this source of power the way to enlighten-ment opens up to her.'

'The way to the absolute freedom?'

'The way to the absolute freedom.'

Yitschak was silent again. The wind became cooler. This time the inner dialogue took a shorter time. 'Sexual attraction possesses beauty and refinement,' he uttered gloomily.

148

'In the same way that the most reliable steel chains which attach a prisoner to the dark wall of his cell possess beauty and refinement.'

'It's very hard to overcome sexual attraction.'

'Without overcoming it completely,' I said, emphasizing the word 'completely', 'there is no way of even considering any kind of freedom whatsoever. Sexual attraction is the most reliable means of enslavement.'

'There were enlightened figures who had sexual relations,' Yitschak informed me. 'Moses for instance.'

'Moses was suited to his era. He had direct contact with the divinity. Enlightenment is recognizing yourself as an inseparable part of the divinity.'

'Is there a difference?'

'Apparently.'

'Nevertheless,' Yitschak insisted, 'the issue of sexual relations has not reached a clear and definite solution – among the great founders of religions as well as among the leaders of various schools!'

'Some of these personalities deliberately avoid discussing the subject, some evade it, and others clearly state that in order to gain freedom, it is essential to overcome sexual attraction completely. If there is absolute triumph over it, there is freedom. If there isn't – there's no freedom.'

'Isn't there any room for an intermediate condition?'

'No.'

'The situation is not very encouraging.'

'If freedom is your wish, you must fight sexual attraction until you destroy it completely. The permissiveness with which the various religions deal with the subject is meant only to attract followers.'

'Aren't those "permissive" religions revealing the truth to their followers?'

'To some of them, they do. In every religion there is a circle for the advanced who are wise and developed people with a well-forged willpower. Those followers are privileged to know the whole truth. Every religion has its own special methods of weaning from sexual attraction. The principal of all methods is constant prayer and contemplation.'

'Only very few distinguished individuals gain true liberation from the mighty enslavement of sexual attraction,' said Yitschak, half asking and half stating.

'Only very few distinguished individuals,' I said.

'And they never cohabit?'

'No, although they alone are allowed to.'

'Why?'

'Because cohabitation cannot re-enslave them to the world of illusion. They are permitted to and the others are not but in reality what happens is the opposite.'

'And in spite of that, they don't cohabit?' persisted Yitschak. 'Why?'

I scrutinised him for a long moment before answering. His eyes were shining and his face expressed great tension.

'Let's presume that you've been hypnotized into licking paper instead of honey and suddenly fortune smiled upon you and you gain liberation from the hypnosis and lick real honey – would you still go back to licking paper?'

Yitschak examined me for a long time. The tension on his face relaxed and his voice too sounded calm when he said, 'I don't see myself as a distinguished individual!'

'You don't need to be in order to fight sexual attraction.'

'It isn't enough to fight,' said Yitschak, 'but to win.'

'The triumph comes by itself; you win if you are diligent in your fight. Sexual attraction falls off you like a withered autumn leaf.'

'And the failures on the way?' asked Yitschak, making a doubtful finger movement.

'They don't count, not in quantity or severity.'

'Then how are you being "diligent" in this fight?'

'You sincerely aspire for release from sexual attraction and – most important of all – you don't stop contemplating.'

'Are sincere aspiration and contemplation enough?'

'Yes.'

'Not every person aspires to be released from sexual attraction,' he said.

'The one who does is destined for liberation. Not every worm aspires to becoming a butterfly; the one that does is the one destined to become a butterfly.'

He thought about it for a minute or two. His head was bent down so that his chin touched his chestbone. Finally, he sighed, lifted his head and said, 'We'll wait and see!'

He stood up and since I remained seated he bid me farewell and went on his way.

151

32

The fable of the railway, the locomotive and its driver

The following week Yitschak did not come to pick me up. The next day, he apologised over the phone that a puncture in one of the car's back tyres had detained him for a considerable time, after which he did not see any point in our meeting. The week after that, he called and informed me in advance that he would not be coming. The third week, he appeared at my workplace somewhat ashamed and asked if he could come into my office. I received him and offered him a cup of tea which was served to me in the morning and had already gone cold and tasteless. He accepted it willingly and drank it thirstily. Apparently something was burning inside him.

'Mr S,' he began, 'you can surely guess...'

'That you don't see any point in continuing our meetings.'

'Not exactly,' he stuttered. 'I want some time to consider and weigh things up in order to come to the right conclusion. Please understand me!'

'It was not I who initiated those meetings.'

'You are absolutely right, but I don't want any misunderstanding here. I'm taking a long leave,' he said and put on a distorted smile. 'I have to make up my mind...' He gazed at me and his eyes pleaded with me to accept his statement just as it was presented, without probing. After a long silence, during which Yitschak's forehead became covered with large drops of sweat while his eyes wandered around in search of more tea that was not available at that hour, I said, 'Please sit beside me!' Though surprised, he hurried to do as I had requested.

'Concentrate for five minutes on the subject, *"What would I like to be?"* and let me know the outcome. He sat up straight the way he had learned. His glance wandered to the wall where a blackboard scribbled with formulas hung. After less than fives minutes he turned to me with an expression of total astonishment and uttered, 'A monk... that is the word that came into my mind!'

'That you will be!' I informed him with a smile.

Yitschak was alarmed. 'Dear sir,' he addressed me in a voice trembling with excitement, 'I'm happy with Eve and intend to marry her; I do not agree to being a monk!'

'But that is what you will be!' I exclaimed and burst into laughter which might have shaken the foundations of the world – had they existed.

'Maybe it was you who planted this in my mind,' Yitschak expressed his suspicion, giving me a contrary look.

'I have no interest whatsoever in doing that!'

'Then how did it happen?'

'Look,' I said, 'do you know what a railway track is?'

He nodded promptly in order to rush me.

'You build the railway track and go on and on for hundreds, sometimes thousands of kilometres. As in Russia or the United States, for example. Do you understand?'

'Go on, man!' Yitschak said with enraged impatience.

'You started getting angry too quickly,' I pointed out. 'It is not to your advantage. Sooner or later you will have to cope with your anger, so you are merely strengthening your enemy now!'

'Mr S, I can hardly follow your speech,' he pleaded. 'I can't grasp the connection between the Siberian train and the spell you've just cast on me.'

'I cast a spell on you?' I stressed my astonishment. 'God forbid, my boy! Remember that I did not mention any Siberian train, I said a *railway track* and as examples I deliberately cited the longest railways.'

'Mr S, you are tormenting me!'

'You've begun getting tormented quickly...' I didn't have time to finish my sentence. Yitschak interrupted, 'What about the train?'

'The railway,' I corrected him calmly. 'The train does not travel before the railway is completed and it makes no difference whether it's the longest or the shortest railway. The point is, it does not travel before its railway track is completed. I find it necessary to stress that fact because it is the keystone of our fable – remember that!' Ignoring a few restless movements by my companion, I continued to relate the fable. 'The train driver who embarks on his first journey does not know what awaits him on his way. For example, he doesn't know exactly what kind of landscape will be revealed to him, how he would cross narrow bridges or whether the tunnels are properly built and will not collapse over his head, burying him underneath. He does not know what awaits him in any of the stations. Still, everything has been planned in advance and he will pass along the very same railway that was designated for him and by no means along a different one or any other! In the light of this fact, the landscape that will be revealed to the driver's eyes will be the landscape along that particular railway and not any other landscape. And so, when the driver wishes to view something with the aid of flashlights or in daylight, he will see nothing other than the designated view which lies along his railway.'

I fell silent in order to give him time to digest my speech and then added, 'You have just peeped at the landscape along your railway and found out what awaits you at your next station!'

'I do not believe in all that chatter!' he protested.

I shrugged my shoulders.

Yitschak lowered his eyes and after a moment of silence, turned to me and said with a hoarse voice, 'Mr S, please, I beg of you, give me your final word of advice! What would I do in order to erase that nightmare?'

'Stop this ugly habit of yours of whimpering! Enough with the advice and support! Your position now is that of a great commander: all your troops are prepared for battle, standing in line and anticipating your signal to attack. On the mountain ridge in front of you the enemy is all set for battle too – no, he is already charging forth. It is quite possible that you'll come out of it safe and sound but maybe only lamentable remains will be left of you. Now if you please, leave me alone! I'm terribly busy!'

And so we parted, not a permanent parting although a prolonged one.

The Author

Shlomo Kalo was born on 25 February 1928 in Sofia, Bulgaria.

From an early age he wrote poems and in 1946 won a prize in a poetry competition. The same year he went to Czecho-slovakia to study medicine in the Karl University in Prague. During this period he also worked as a freelance journalist and wrote short stories.

When the State of Israel was founded he joined M.A.H.A.L. and was sent to Holomotz to train as a pilot. On 1 January 1949 he emigrated to Israel. In 1958 he was awarded M.Sc. in microbiology by the University of Tel-Aviv.

From 1962 until his retirement in 1982, he was the director of medical laboratories at the General Health Services (*Kupat Holim Klalit*) of Rishon le Zion.

Until 1969 he continued his literary activities at a leisurely pace. He translated many of the classics of world religions such as the *Bhagavad Gita, Tao Te Ching, Fables,* and others. During this period he published *The Catacombs,* Sifriat Hapoalim, 1954; *The Heap,* Am Oved, 1962; *The Heart of Flesh,* Am Oved, 1966.

The sharp turning point in his life which occurred in the first week of 1969 is reflected in the prolific literary activity that followed. *The Self as Fighter* (1979), *The Dauntless* (1981), *Dialogue of Freedom* (1982), *Thou Art Thou* (1984), *Journey to Athos* [the continuation of *The Self as Fighter*] (1985), *The Art of War for True Freedom* (1986), *The Gospel of the Absolute Free Will* (1987), *My Friends & As a Scarlet Thread,* (1988), *Truth Is Bliss – Lectures of the Master & A People of Chiefs – Lectures of the Master* (1989), *Son of Another Star & The Victory of Love – Lectures of the Master* (1990) all published by D.A.T. [DAT in Hebrew means knowledge, and is also the initials of three other words which mean: know yourself always.] *The Self as Fighter* is the first book by Shlomo Kalo to be translated into English.

The Translator

Anat Rekem was born on 8 April 1959 in Tel-Aviv, Israel. She grew up in Genossar – a kibbutz by the Sea of Galilee – and studied music.

When she had completed the two years' obligatory military service in the Israeli Army (1977-79) she went and settled herself in Tel-Aviv where in 1982 she took up a career as a professional singer. Success in her professional activity demanded extensive travels in Europe; this made her take up residence in Belgium.

In 1986 she became acquainted with the works of Shlomo Kalo. In May 1987 the author suggested that she undertake the translation of his works into English.

ACKNOWLEDGEMENTS: The translator would like to express her profound gratitude to: Beverley Dean for her encouragement and willingness to help, and for her valuable advice and suggestions regarding style; Gidon Lana who kindly read the first draft, made a number of useful suggestions and helped with the biblical quotations; Amos Rosen and Diana de Smedt for reading through and offering suggestions for improving the translation; Jacky Kahan for his assistance with the computer work, his constant help and support and his invaluable friendship.